Everything Oz

MAKE MUNCHKIN PLACECARDS,
OVER THE RAINBOW CAKE,
"I'M MELTING" WITCH CANDLES,
AND MUCH MORE

CHRISTINE LEECH
HANNAH READ-BALDREY

CHICAGO
REVIEW
PRESS

30

19

10

74

Dress-Up Dorothy

38

92

66

Munchkin Place Cards

58

The Cowardly Lion Hand Puppet

Poppy T-Shirt

WITHDRAWN

OOGABOO

Winkie
Country

Quadling
Country

China Country

Palace of Glinda the Good

OF OZ

G

YIPS

JINXLAND

OZ

HONI SOIT QVI MAL Y PEASE

Creative Directors **Christine Leech & Hannah Read-Baldrey**
Art Director & Designer **Christine Leech**
Stylist & Illustrator **Hannah Read-Baldrey**
Photographer **Verity Welstead**

For Quadrille Publishing
Editorial Director **Jane O'Shea**
Creative Director **Helen Lewis**
Project Editor **Lisa Pendreigh**
Design Assistant **Nicola Davidson**
Production Director **Vincent Smith**
Production Controller **James Finan**

First published in 2012 by
Quadrille Publishing Ltd.
Alhambra House
27–31 Charing Cross Road
London WC2H 0LS
www.quadrille.co.uk

Quadrille
craft

Chicago Review Press, Incorporated
814 North Franklin Street
Chicago, Illinois 60610
ISBN 978-1-61374-810-7
Printed in China

CONTENTS

Roll up! Roll up!
COME JOIN US
✶ ✶ ✶ ✶ ✶ ✶ ✶ *and the* ✶ ✶ ✶ ✶ ✶ ✶ ✶ ✶ ✶ ✶ ✶ ✶ ✶ ✶
WONDERFUL WIZARD OF OZ

Welcome to *Everything Oz*. Whether you are a mischievous Munchkin or a beautiful Good Witch, we hope you enjoy this journey down the Yellow Brick Road!

Following the success of our first book, *Everything Alice*, we are delighted to take *The Wonderful Wizard of Oz* as the theme of this follow-up book. Determined to do this much-loved tale justice, we have had fun gathering together ideas based on the original

Chicken Catcher Verity

book, as well as taking inspiration from the many stage and film adaptations.

After creating the projects and testing the recipes, the first part of the photoshoot took place in a London studio on possibly the hottest day of the year.

Hannah designed and built a set with a traveling show theme to fit the theatrical style of the late nineteenth century, when the original book was written.

We loved shooting the green-painted Emerald City Confectionery Cart (see page 85), which was adorned with delicious candy delights. The giant paper Field-O-Poppies (see pages 64–67) was so beautiful we didn't want to take it down. It took us a very late night to prepare them and, once dusted with a sprinkling of magical glitter, they seemed as though they were straight out of a movie.

Alongside photographer Verity, we risked working not only with an animal but also a child! We kept it in the family with Hannah's gorgeous nephew Christian, who modeled the supercute Little Monkey Baby's Bath Towel (see pages 112–14). The fabulous Maggie—aka Toto—is Hannah's

sister-in-law's Miniature Schnauzer, who showed off the stylish Best-in-Show Toto's Jacket (see pages 98–99) to perfection. Maggie was so well behaved, she could be a professional model!

Then it was off to East Sussex. The farm we shot at is just down the road from the home of Christine's parents. It has a very traditional Victorian feel to it and is full of chickens, pigs, and barking dogs. The resident peacock had a serious bee in his bonnet against Verity's car, which left with several scratches! We have to say a big thank you to the owners Mr. and Mrs. Peters.

At the farm we had planned to shoot outside, but that was when it rained . . . and rained . . . and rained. So lights were wrapped in plastic bags, rigged outside under umbrellas, and shone

CHRISTINE SAYS . . .

I remember reading *The Wonderful Wizard of Oz* curled up on my bed. The gray opening chapters didn't seem too promising at first, but when the cyclone came and whisked Dorothy off to the Land of Oz, I went with her . . . Dorothy enthralled me, the Munckhins made me laugh, the Winged Monkeys frightened me, and the whole book transported me to a wonderful world of make-believe.

A very wet Christine

✱ A BRIEF HISTORY OF OZ

through the windows of outhouses to simulate daylight. Meanwhile, we were head-to-toe in rain gear—all looking like three damp Dorothys!

Over the few days we were at the farm, thankfully the weather did improve and we got some fabulous outside shots such as the The No-Brainer Scarecrow (see pages 42–43). We made some little orange feathered friends along the way . . . well, Verity did. We were determined to get a hen in the photograph of Dorothy's Raffia Flower Basket (pages 44–46); hilariously, only Verity was confident enough to catch one, so she was nicknamed the Chicken Catcher!

Once all the shots were taken, it was time to head back to London. Christine set about designing the pages of the book and Hannah creating the illustrations. We can truly say we adore this book and hope you too are whisked away into a magical world of your own.

A love of the theater is where this story begins, L. Frank Baum, author of *The Wonderful Wizard of Oz*, was infatuated by the stage.

Born in 1856 in Chittenango, New York, Baum was a kind man with a generous nature. With the help of his father, Baum founded a theater in 1880 and set about writing plays.

Sadly the theater burned to the ground, ironically while the show *Matches* was playing. Devastated by the loss of his scripts and costumes in the fire, Baum moved to South Dakota with his new wife. At the time the area was drought ridden; his later depiction of Kansas was based on this experience. He attempted many business ventures, several of which nearly bankrupted him. He ran Baum's Bazaar, but his generosity with credit led to the store's demise. Following these failures, Baum started to write down the nursery rhymes he improvised and told to his sons over the years. *Mother Goose in Prose* was published in 1897 to immediate success. In 1899 he collaborated with illustrator W.W. Denslow on *Father Goose: His Book*, which met with rave reviews and became a bestseller.

The year 1900 saw the publication of another collaboration between Baum and Denslow, *The Wonderful Wizard of Oz*, which was met with great acclaim and adapted as a musical for Broadway in 1903. Baum met the demand for the first book by continuing a series of Oz stories.

A move to Hollywood and three more successful books followed in 1910, however in 1911 Baum was declared bankrupt. He began the Oz Film Manufacturing Company, experimenting with film effects, but the company folded after a year.

After years of failing health, Baum died in 1919. He is buried in the Forest Lawn Memorial Park Cemetery in Glendale, California.

CRAFT ESSENTIALS

★★★★★★★★★★★★★★★★★★★★★★★★★★★★

A good craft kit is like a magpie's nest: full of little scraps of fabric, paper, and sparkly things that may just be put to use one day.

- Scissors: *Never mix up your scissors for cutting paper with your scissors for cutting fabric; they will stay sharper for longer if they do only one job. Small embroidery scissors are useful for snipping stray threads, and pinking shears create decorative edges.*
- Craft knife
- Wire cutters
- Glue: *White craft glue is useful as an adhesive and a sealant. A glue gun, glues for fabric, paper glue, and superglue are also handy. Glue dots come in all shapes and sizes and using them is a clean and easy way to attach things.*
- Tapes: *Invisible, masking, and duct.*

- Staple gun or stapler
- Brass paper fasteners
- Sewing machine
- Sewing needles: *A good selection of needles with various size holes and thicknesses, including ones for embroidery. A big blunt needle with a large eye is very useful for threading ribbon or elastic through hems.*
- Pins
- Threads: *Various cotton and silk threads for sewing and embroidery.*
- Tailor's chalk or a dressmaker's disappearing-ink pen
- Tape measure & steel ruler
- Assorted paintbrushes

COOKERY ESSENTIALS

★★★★★★★★★★★★★★★★★★★★★★★★★★★★★★

*Good quality cookery utensils will not only last you
years but also help you achieve perfect results.*

- Measuring cups
- Measuring spoons
- Wooden spoons
- Kitchen scale
- Sifter
- Whisk: *Electric, balloon, or food processor.*
- Rubber spatula: *Perfect for cleaning bowls.*
- Rolling pin
- Mixing bowls: *Big ones for cakes and small ones for frosting.*
- Baking sheet: *Best with edges, for extra grip when removing from a hot oven.*

- Cupcake or muffin pan
- Cake pans
- Foil, plastic wrap, & parchment paper
- Cooling rack
- Wooden cocktail sticks
- Paper cupcake cases
- Pastry bags: *Disposable plastic ones are best to reduce mess.*
- Pastry-bag tips: *A ³/₈″ nozzle for crullers and a selection of smaller star and writing tips for decoration.*
- Knives: *Bread knife and other sharp knives.*

DRESS-UP DOROTHY & TOTO

with apron, basket, & lion mask

✶✶✶✶✶✶✶✶✶✶✶✶✶✶✶✶✶✶✶✶✶✶✶✶✶✶✶✶✶✶

Dorothy, of course, is the star of the show, so she needs a celebrity wardrobe! Accessorize this delightful doll with her very own gingham apron, straw basket, and costume-party lion mask. Accompanied by her faithful companion, Toto, Dorothy is ready for any occasion.

YOU WILL NEED

For Dorothy
- 8" x 12" of white cotton fabric
- 8" x 16" of blue-and-white gingham cotton fabric
- 12" x 12" of black-and-white striped cotton fabric
- 9" x 12" of brown wool felt
- Scraps of wool felt in both white and red
- Matching sewing threads
- Black, dark pink or red, and pale pink coloring pens, with medium-sized tips, for face
- Toy stuffing
- Wooden spoon
- Two small buttons

For Toto
- 9" x 12" of black wool felt
- 5" x 5" of ³⁄₄"-thick batting
- Matching sewing thread
- 10" length of narrow red ribbon

For the basket
- 9" x 12" of brown felt
- Scraps of red and green felt
- Matching sewing thread

✶ Using the templates on page 126, cut the following from the white fabric: one head and four arms. Cut the following from the gingham fabric: two bodies. Cut the following from the striped fabric: two front and two back legs. Cut the following from brown felt: one back head and one front hair. Cut the following from red felt: two front and two back shoes. Cut the following from white felt: one front and back collar.

✶ To create Dorothy's face, simply lay the brown front hair over the white head to frame her face. Then draw her facial features onto the white cotton using the pens. We used black for her eyes and nose, then dark pink for her lips. Next, we dabbed dots of pale pink pen onto our fingers, which we then pressed onto the fabric to color her cheeks (1). It is a good idea to draw Dorothy's face before you start sewing as it can sometimes go wrong; this way it is easy to replace this piece if you are dissatisfied with the results.

join the head to the body

✶ Once you are happy with Dorothy's features, stitch the brown front hair around the drawn face. Topstitch approximately ¹⁄₄" inside the edge of her hairline: if you are feeling adventurous, create some swirly locks of hair with extra lines of stitching.

✶ To make the body, stitch the front and back white felt collars to the two body pieces along the neck edge. Hem the bottom edges of the body. Stitch the bottom edge of the head and the back of head to the correct body pieces, ensuring that the seam is facing inward (2).

✶ To make the legs, position one red felt shoe on the foot of each leg. Baste in place. With right sides together, sew the legs together in pairs, leaving the top edge open. Turn right side out. Fill firmly with toy stuffing, packing evenly from the toes upward using the round-ended handle of a wooden spoon (3).

join the arms

3

stuff the legs

4

6

5

7

9

Dorothy in her gingham apron

★ Make the arms in the same way as the legs. Baste the arms to the body, with the arms facing inward (4).

★ Braid together three 6"-x-$\frac{1}{2}$" lengths of brown felt, securing the ends with a few stitches. Repeat for the second braid. Position each braid, facing inward, on the head, and baste in place.

★ Place the joined head and body pieces with right sides together. Stitch all around the outside edges, leaving the hem of the dress open. Turn right side out, then stuff (5).

★ Position the legs inside the dress hem, curving inward. Stitch to close the hem.

★ Sew a button to the collar. Stitch the braids into loops and add a red felt poppy.

TOTO

★ Fold the felt in half, sandwiching the batting in between. Pin together.

★ Using the Toto template on page 127, trace the outline onto the felt. Sew zigzag stitches all around the outline. Trim the excess felt close to the line of stitches.

★ Tie a length of red ribbon into a bow around his neck and trim the ends.

BASKET

★ Using the template on page 127, cut the following from the brown felt: two basket sides. Also cut one $\frac{5}{8}$"-x-6$\frac{3}{4}$" strip for the handle and one 2"-x-8$\frac{3}{4}$" rectangle for the base.

★ Stitch one long side of the base to one basket side, curving it around the bottom corners. Repeat for the second side. Turn right side out.

★ Position the ends of the handle centrally on opposite sides of the basket. Secure with reinforced stitching.

★ Place a piece of cardboard in the base of the basket if it needs stiffening.

★ Add a simple appliqué felt apple and leaves to one side of the basket.

LION MASK

YOU WILL NEED

- 9" x 12" of wool felt in each of yellow and orange
- Scraps of cream and black wool felt
- Matching sewing thread
- Fabric glue

✶ Using the templates on page 127, cut the following from yellow felt: one head and two ears. Cut the following from orange felt: one mane and one head. Cut the following from cream felt: one muzzle. Cut the following from black felt: two eyes, one nose, one mouth, and four whiskers.

✶ Position the muzzle on the yellow head. Secure with zigzag stitches. Using glue, add the eyes, nose, mouth, and whiskers. Pinch the ears in the middle and pin to the edge of the head.

✶ Snip along the mane, where marked on the template. Position the mane in between the yellow and orange heads. Stitch all around the sides, securing the mane and ears in place, but leaving the bottom edge open.

GINGHAM APRON

YOU WILL NEED

- 20" x 12" of blue-and-white gingham
- 2" length of narrow white lace
- Matching sewing thread
- Red embroidery thread

✶ Using the templates on page 127, cut one apron and one pocket from the gingham fabric. Also cut one 2"-x-20" strip for the waistband and one 1½"-x-6¼" strip for the neck strap.

✶ Turn under, press, and topstitch a ³⁄₈" hem all around the apron. Fold both the waistband and strap in half lengthwise. Turn under and press a ³⁄₈" hem along the long edges. Stitch all the way around. Stitch the ends of the strap to the sides of the bib and the waistband centrally across the apron.

✶ Along the curved side of the pocket, clip notches into the seam allowance. Turn under, press, and topstitch a ³⁄₈" hem all around. Position the pocket on the apron skirt, pin, and work neat blanket stitches in red embroidery thread around the curve.

✶ Trim the neck edge and the hem of the apron with lengths of white lace.

Aunt Em's
FRENCH CRULLERS

☆ ☆

Kansas is a mighty fine place to try French-influenced desserts. Aunt Em's family recipe has been passed down through generations; consider yourself lucky she has shared it here!

YOU WILL NEED

- 1 cup whole milk
- ½ cup water
- ½ cup plus 1 tablespoon superfine sugar
- ½ teaspoon salt
- ½ cup unsalted butter
- 1½ cups self-raising flour
- Few drops of vanilla extract
- 4 extra-large eggs, beaten

For the glaze
- 2¼ cups powdered sugar, sifted
- 2 tablespoons maple syrup
- 2 tablespoons milk

You will also need a pastry bag fitted with a ³⁄₈" star tip.

Makes 12 crullers

☆ Preheat the oven to 400°F.

☆ Cut two pieces of parchment paper to the size of your baking sheets. Using a 4"-diameter mug, draw six pencil circles onto each piece of parchment paper, spacing them about 1¼" apart. Turn over the parchment so the pencil marks are on the underside. Place on the baking sheets.

☆ Pour the milk and water into a deep saucepan. Add the sugar, salt, and butter and place over a medium heat. Stir continuously with a wooden spoon until the butter has melted. Turn up the heat and bring the mixture to a boil. Add the vanilla extract.

☆ Add the flour all at once. Continue stirring briskly with a wooden spoon until the mixture forms a ball and leaves the sides of the pan clean. Beat vigorously for 1–2 minutes before removing from the heat. Transfer to a ceramic or glass bowl and leave to cool for 5 minutes.

☆ Add the eggs one at a time, beating with a wooden spoon. Once the egg is incorporated, the paste will be thick and glossy.

☆ Spoon the mixture into a pastry bag fitted with a ³⁄₈" star tip. Using the pencil marks as a guide, pipe equal rounds onto the parchment paper.

☆ Bake for 15 minutes. Reduce the oven temperature to 375°F and bake for 20 minutes more or until the pastries are golden brown. The crullers will really puff up, almost doubling in size. Once baked, place on a wire rack to cool.

For the glaze
☆ Place the powdered sugar, maple syrup, and milk together in a bowl. Mix until thick, glossy, and there are no lumps.

☆ Slide a piece of parchment paper underneath the wire rack. Brush or spoon the glaze over the crullers (1). Sprinkle with a little more icing sugar before serving.

brush or spoon over the glaze

Faithful Friend

TOTO PILLOW

★ ★

This ultra-soft pillow puts to good use any old sweaters you may have lying around. Wool knit fabric with a cashmere content is super snuggly.

YOU WILL NEED

- 25" wide x 40" long of white fabric for lining
- Two pieces 19" x 25" of wool knit fabric, such as from an old sweater, for outer cover
- Matching sewing thread
- Dressmaker's disappearing-ink pen or tailor's chalk
- Wooden spoon
- Toy stuffing
- Two ³/₄" circles of black or brown wool felt for eyes
- Gingham scarf or napkin for bow

Note: If you are using an old sweater, cut away the neck and arms only to create rectangles of fabric. Do not cut down the sides of the sweater. Leaving the seams intact makes it easier to keep everything in place when sewing the pillow together.

By making two pillows—one from lining fabric and one from a stretchy wool knit fabric—you will achieve a better dog shape.

★ Fold the white lining fabric in half widthwise, with right sides together, and pin. Using the template on page 128, trace the outline onto the fabric. Machine stitch around the outline, leaving a 4" opening along the dog's underbelly. Trim the excess fabric ¹/₂" from the line of stitching (1).

★ Clip notches in the seam allowance of the fabric along the curves around the ears, nose, tail, and legs (2). This will create a better overall shape and neater curves.

★ Turn the lining right side out. Using the handle of a wooden spoon, open out all the curves, such as the tip of the tail. Press.

★ Repeat the previous steps but this time using the wool knit outer-cover fabric. As the knit fabric will be quite stretchy, stitch slightly inside the outline to avoid a misshapen Toto (3).

★ Turn the outer cover right side out and carefully insert the shaped lining. Make sure the ears, nose, tail, and legs are all aligned and lay flat.

★ Firmly fill the pillow with toy stuffing, pushing it into all the extremities. Close both of the openings with neat hand stitches.

★ Sew on a small circle of black or brown felt to either side of the head for eyes.

★ Finally spruce up Toto by tying a gingham scarf or napkin into a pretty bow around his neck.

notch the curved seams

Uncle Henry's Famous CHERRY PIE

✶ ✶

For a time it was illegal to serve ice cream with cherry pie in Kansas.
This recipe is so good, it is practically criminal!

YOU WILL NEED

For the pastry

- 2 cups all-purpose flour
- 2 tablespoons powdered sugar
- Large pinch of salt
- ¾ cup unsalted butter, chilled
- ¾ cup cream cheese
- ¼–⅓ cup light cream

For the filling

- 2 pounds 4 ounces unpitted sweet cherries (or 2 pounds 14 ounces if pitted)
- Juice of half a small lemon
- ¾ cup superfine sugar
- 1 heaped teaspoon ground cinnamon
- 3 rounded tablespoons cornstarch

You will also need a 9" round deep pie pan or shallow tart pan.

To make the pastry dough

✶ Sift the flour, powdered sugar, and salt together into a bowl.

✶ Cut the chilled butter into small dice and add to the flour with the cream cheese. Using your fingertips, rub the butter into the flour until it resembles coarse breadcrumbs.

✶ Pour in the cream a little at a time until the mixture forms a soft dough. Gather the dough into a ball and knead briefly to smooth out any lumps.

✶ Divide the dough equally into two pieces and chill for at least 1 hour or overnight.

To make the cherry filling

✶ If unpitted, remove the stones from the cherries. Sprinkle them with the lemon juice, superfine sugar, cinnamon, and cornstarch. Gently combine until all the cherries are covered in the syrup. Leave to stand for at least 20 minutes, then stir once more.

✶ On a floured surface, roll out half the dough and use to line a 9" pie pan or shallow tart pan. Roll out the remaining dough to a 9" circle for the pie lid and place on a sheet of parchment paper. Chill both the dough-lined pie pan and the lid until ready to bake.

✶ Preheat the oven to 425°F.

✶ Pile the cherries into the dough-lined pie dish to form a gently swelling mound. Brush the edges of the pie crust with water, then lay the lid on top. Crimp the edges firmly together with the tines of a fork. Trim any excess pastry. Cut a hole or holes in the pie lid to allow steam to escape. You can also add decorative pastry shapes to the lid using any excess dough.

✶ Bake for 20 minutes. Reduce the oven temperature to 350°F and bake for 30–40 minutes more or until the cherry juice bubbles up through the steam holes. If the pie crust is darkening too quickly, cover loosely with aluminum foil.

✶ Serve the cherry pie warm in slices with vanilla ice cream.

FRILL DRAPE

✶✶✶✶✶✶✶✶✶✶✶✶✶✶✶✶✶✶✶✶✶✶✶✶✶✶✶✶✶✶✶✶✶

*This girly drape looks just as stunning in a bedroom or living room as it does in a barn.
The delicate hues of each frill can be made more or less subtle to suit a variety of décors.*

YOU WILL NEED

- A ready-made plain white drape in a width to cover your window
- Seven pieces of different color plain or print cotton fabrics, in a size to suit your drape (see instructions)
- Matching sewing thread
- Dressmaker's disappearing-ink pen
- 1-yard-long metal ruler

Note: The hem allowance is $5/8$" throughout.

✶ Measure the height of the window where the frill drape will be hung. Using this measurement, hem the ready-made drape accordingly to create the required drop.

✶ To calculate the amount of each colored fabric that you will need, multiply the width of the ready-made drape by $2^{1/2}$ and add $1^{1/4}$". This gives you your first measurement. Next, divide the length of the ready-made drape by 7 and add $3^{1/4}$". This gives you your second measurement. The additional $3^{1/4}$" allows for both a 2" overlap of each frill and the hem allowances.

✶ Turn under, press, and topstitch a $5/8$" hem on all sides of the seven pieces of cotton.

fold and pin the box pleats

✶ With a disappearing-ink pen and metal ruler, lightly mark a guideline for where each colored frill will be stitched onto the ready-made drape. This helps to maintain a straight line when sewing. Do not forget that each frill should overhang the one below it by 2".

✶ Lay out the ready-made drape on a clean floor. Beginning at the top edge, position the first frill along its sewing guideline and pin into a series of box pleats. We made five box pleats across the width of each of our frills. To make a box pleat, fold the fabric so that the two upper folds of the pleat face in opposite directions, while the two under folds are laid toward each other (1). Stitch the frill in place along the guideline (2).

✶ Repeat for all the subsequent frills until the last one is in place and covers the bottom edge of the ready-made drape.

✶ Trim any loose threads, press, and hang.

BLUEBIRD WREATH

Somewhere over the rainbow, bluebirds fly! What could be more joyful than this chirpy all-seasons wreath? The bright wool-wrapped ring brings sparkle to a wall or door.

YOU WILL NEED

- 14" polystyrene foam half-ring wreath
- Three balls wool yarn in different colors
- Hot-glue gun
- Selection of brightly colored felt for flowers
- Selection of trimmings, such as decorative buttons, flower appliqués, gems, and pearl bud sprigs
- Decorative bluebirds

Note: For indoor use only.

✶ With the ends to the back, wrap the yarn closely around the polystyrene foam wreath (1). Vary the widths of each section. The thicker the yarn, the less time this stage takes.

✶ To create decorative flowers, cut out six petal shapes from felt. Dot a blob of glue on one end of each petal and pinch into shape (2). Join them all together using a hot-glue gun, then add a button or gem to the center.

✶ Vary the petal shapes to create different flowers (3). Arrange all your felt flowers and trimmings around the wreath. Once you find your preferred arrangement, hot-glue them in place on the wreath.

✶ Finally, also hot-glue your bluebirds to the wreath, nestled in the felt flowers (4).

Dorothy's PATCHWORK APRON

✶ ✶

This patchwork apron is great for using up all your rainbow-colored scraps of fabric.

To make the apron

✶ Place the plain cotton apron front on the print cotton apron back with right sides together. Pin together and fold in half lengthwise (parallel to the 22" sides). With tailor's chalk, mark the points 12" down from the top edge and 8" in from the side. Draw and cut a gentle curve between these two marks through all the fabric layers (1).

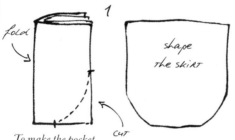

To make the pocket

✶ Cut 4"-wide rectangles of varying lengths—but no longer than 10"—from different print fabrics. Stitch these together with ³⁄₈" seam allowances to create a patchwork piece that is at least 26" x 10".

✶ Place the patchwork pocket piece on the plain cotton pocket back with right sides together. Stitch all the way around leaving a small opening along the base of the rectangle. Turn right side out and press.

✶ Place the plain front on top of the print back and place the pocket between these two layers, aligning the bottom edges. Make sure the plain pocket back is face up and the edge with the opening is at the bottom. The square corners of the pocket piece will extend beyond the curved edges of the apron skirt. Pin all the layers together (2).

✶ Starting at one top corner and following the curved lines, stitch down the side and around the apron skirt up to the opposite corner, leaving the top edge open. Trim the corners of the pocket piece into curves. Turn right side out and press. To create divisions in the pocket, stitch along a few of the vertical seams of the patchwork.

✶ Using a length of embroidery thread, sew a line of loose running stitch along the top edge. Gently gather the fabric to a width of 16¹⁄₂" and secure the thread at either side (3).

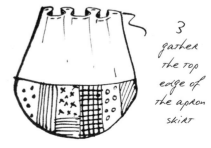

To make the tie

✳ The apron tie wraps around the waist and makes a bow at the front: it is 3¼ yards long.

✳ Cut about thirty 4"-wide rectangles of varying lengths—but no longer than 12" and no shorter than 4"—from different print fabrics. Divide the rectangles in two equal piles with a similar number of long and short pieces. This is to ensure the front and back of the tie are the same length.

✳ Cut four 6"-wide rectangles that are 8" in length from different print fabrics. This is to ensure the end sections of the tie are slightly wider than the rest.

✳ Using one of the piles, stitch two rectangles together along the short edge. Repeat this until all the pieces are joined in pairs. Next, stitch two pairs together along one short edge. Repeat this until all your rectangles are joined together to create one long tie. As you sew, check the length of the tie by wrapping it around your waist. Once it reaches your preferred length, join a set of 6"-wide rectangles to each end of the tie. Repeat with the second pile of rectangles, matching the length to the first tie. Press each tie piece.

✳ Place the tie pieces with right sides together. Fold in half to find the mid-point of the tie. Mark points 8¼" either side of the mid-point for an opening for the apron skirt.

✳ Starting at a marked point and

working outward, stitch all the way around the tie to the second marked point. As you stitch gradually widen the tie at the ends and stitch a diagonal

rather than vertical line up the short sides (4). Turn right side out and press. Turn under and press a neat hem along the opening.

✳ Insert the top of the apron into the tie opening, spreading the gathers evenly across the width. Pin and topstitch the tie opening closed and the apron skirt in place (5). Tie a bow at the front when wearing (6).

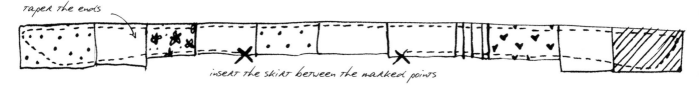

taper the ends

insert the skirt between the marked points

LAST EDITION

The Kansas Daily Tribune.

VOLUME XXXVII   WICHITA, KANSAS JUNE 4. 1890   TUESDAY MORNING

WINDSWEPT!
GIRL TAKEN BY CYCLONE

DOROTHY GALE RETURNS FROM GREAT TWISTER ADVENTURE

Speaking exclusively to the *Kansas Daily Tribune* on her return, Dorothy Gale tells of her experiences RIGHT AT THE HEART OF THE CYCLONE!

"Well, the house whirled around two or three times and rose slowly through the air. I felt as if I were going up in a balloon."

In a freak of nature the north and south winds met where the house stood, and made it the exact center of the cyclone. According to experts in the middle of a cyclone the air is generally still, but the great pressure of the wind on every side of the house raised it up higher and higher, until it was at the very top of the cyclone; and there it remained and was carried miles and miles away as easily as you could carry a feather.

"It was very dark, and the wind howled horribly around me," Dorothy continues, "but I found I was riding quite easily. After the first few whirls around, and one other time when the house tipped badly, I felt as if I were being rocked gently, like a baby in a cradle."

TOTO'S FEARS

"Toto did not like it. He ran about the room, now here, now there, barking loudly; but I sat quite still on the floor and waited to see what would happen."

"Once Toto got too near the open trap door, and fell in; and at first I thought I had lost him. But soon I saw one of his ears sticking up through the hole. Experts tell me the strong pressure of the air was keeping him up so that he could not fall. I crept to the hole, caught Toto by the ear, and dragged him into the room again, afterward closing the trap door so that no more accidents could happen."

ALL ALONE

"Hour after hour passed away, and slowly I got over my fright; but I felt quite lonely, and the wind shrieked so loudly all about me that I nearly became deaf. At first I had wondered if I would be dashed to pieces when the house fell again; but as the hours passed and nothing terrible happened, I stopped worrying and resolved to wait calmly and see what the future would bring. At last I crawled over the swaying floor to my bed, and lay down upon it; and Toto followed and lay down beside me."

"In spite of the swaying of the house and the wailing of the wind, I soon closed my eyes and fell fast asleep."

HOME SWEET HOME

Dorothy declines to comment on what happened after this but she does say, "This trip has taught me there is no place like home."

CYCLONE CUPCAKES

****

Get swept away by these luscious lemon cupcakes with a mini-meringue tornado topping

YOU WILL NEED

For the cupcakes
- ⅓ cup plus 1 tablespoon unsalted butter, softened
- ½ cup superfine sugar
- Zest of 1 lemon, finely grated
- 2 large eggs, lightly beaten
- ⅔ cup self-raising flour, sifted
- ¼ teaspoon baking powder

For the filling
- Jar of lemon curd

For the meringue topping
- 2 large egg whites
- ⅔ cup superfine sugar

Makes 12 cupcakes

To make the cupcakes

✶ Preheat the oven to 350°F. Line a 12-hole cupcake pan with paper liners.

✶ Place the butter, sugar, and grated lemon zest in a bowl and, using either a wooden spoon or an electric mixer, cream together until light and fluffy.

✶ Add the beaten egg gradually, mixing well after each addition.

✶ Once all the egg has been incorporated into the butter mixture, fold in the sifted flour and baking powder and stir until just combined. This will ensure that the cupcakes stay light and fluffy.

✶ Bake in the oven for 15 to 20 minutes, depending on your oven. After 10 minutes, check the cupcakes by inserting a wooden cocktail stick into the middle. If it comes out clean, they are cooked. If it comes out covered in crumbs, bake for a few minutes more. To stop the cupcakes from drying out, do not overcook at this stage as they will go back in the oven later.

To make the meringue
Even the smallest speck of grease or fat in the egg whites or on the bowl or utensils can affect how stiffly egg whites whip up. Make sure you separate the eggs carefully, use a superclean whisk and a glass or metal bowl. Eggs that are a couple of days old used at room temperature create stiffer peaks.

✶ Using an electric whisk set to medium, beat the egg whites until stiff peaks form in the bowl. (A hand balloon whisk is fine, too, it just takes longer and is much more tiring.)

✶ Gradually add the sugar to the egg whites, whisking constantly until the mixture turns glossy with a silky consistency. The meringue is ready when the peaks hold their shape rather than flop over—or when you can hold the bowl upside down over your head and nothing falls out!

To decorate the cupcakes
✶ Place a small teaspoon of lemon curd in the center of each cupcake.

✶ Transfer the meringue mixture into a pastry bag fitted with a round tip. Pipe meringue whirlwinds on top of each cake, completely covering the lemon curd.

✶ Return to the oven for approximately 10 minutes or until the meringue is golden brown and firm to the touch.

✶ Leave on a wire rack to cool. Eat the cupcakes within two days.

SQUASHED WITCH CUPCAKES

✳ ✳

Take a leaf out of Dorothy's book and be sure to squash all the bad witches. The difference with these Squashed Witch Cupcakes is they leave a totally delicious taste in your mouth!

YOU WILL NEED

For the cupcakes
- ³/₄ cup plus 1 tablespoon self-raising flour
- ¹/₂ teaspoon baking powder
- ¹/₂ teaspoon baking soda
- ¹/₃ cup unsweetened cocoa powder
- ¹/₂ teaspoon salt
- 2 tablespoons unsalted butter, softened
- 1 cup plus 2 tablespoons superfine sugar
- 1 large egg, lightly beaten
- Few drops of vanilla extract
- ³/₄ cup whole milk

For the decoration
- Small amounts of white, black, green, and red ready-made rolled fondant icing
- Wooden skewer
- Edible red glitter
- Powdered sugar for dusting
- Cake glue or egg white
- Apricot jam

Makes 12 cupcakes

To make the cupcakes

✳ Preheat oven to 350°F. Line a 12-hole cupcake pan with foil liners.

✳ Sift the flour, baking powder and soda, cocoa, and salt together into a bowl. Place the butter and sugar in a separate bowl and cream together until light and fluffy. Add the vanilla extract. Add the beaten egg gradually, mixing well after each addition.

✳ Once the egg has been incorporated, fold in the sifted dry ingredients a few spoonfuls at a time, alternating with the milk.

✳ Fill the cases three-quarters full only with the mixture. Bake for 15–18 minutes or until a wooden toothpick inserted in the middle comes out clean. Leave to cool on a wire rack then store in an airtight container.

To decorate

✳ For each leg, roll out an 3¹/₄" length of white fondant icing about ¹/₄" thick. Repeat with the black icing, but roll it to half the thickness. To create the stripes, lay one end of the black icing on the white at an angle and then roll, pressing lightly as you go (1).

✳ For each shoe, roll out a ³/₄" ball of red icing, then flatten it slightly. Make a small indentation where the leg fits into the shoe and then shape the other end into a point for the toe. Using cake glue or egg white, secure a striped leg to each shoe. Shape the shoe's heel using a wooden skewer (2). Sprinkle with edible red glitter (3). Leave the legs and shoes to harden overnight.

✳ Lightly dust a work surface with powdered sugar. Roll out the green icing to a thickness of ¹/₈". Using a round serrated cookie cutter slightly wider that the tops of the cupcakes, press out twelve green skirts.

✳ To assemble, for each cake place a small circle of parchment paper on your serving plate and sit a pair of legs on top. Brush a thin layer of apricot jam on the tops of the legs and lay a green skirt over the legs. Brush another layer of jam over the skirt, place an upside-down cupcake on top, and gently press.

Wicked Witch *of the* East's
RUBY SLIPPERS

✴ ✴

There's no place like home! Transform old heels into a magical pair of Ruby Slippers. Using easy elasticized trim, create shoes with minimum mess and maximum durability.

YOU WILL NEED

- Pair of heeled shoes, cleaned
- Bright red or metallic silver spray paint
- Old newspaper
- Hot-glue gun
- 4½ yards of red or silver elasticized sequin trim, 1" wide

✴ In a well-ventilated space (preferably outdoors), spray paint the shoes either red or silver. Use sheets of old newspaper to protect surfaces from the paint. There is no need to paint the insides or soles. Leave to air dry.

start adding the sequins

✴ Beginning at the back of the shoe, just above the heel, attach one end of the elasticized sequin trim to the upper using the hot-glue gun (1). Working around the bottom edge of the shoe, gluing as you proceed, completely cover the shoe's upper with rows of the sequin trim (2).

✴ Once the upper is fully covered, wrap the shoe's heel in the sequin trim beginning at the bottom and working up to the top.

✴ To make a bow, cut an 8" length of sequin trim. Fold both ends inward and fix in the middle with glue to create two bow loops. Cut a shorter 2½" length of sequin trim and wrap it around the middle of the bow to cover the center join. Glue a bow to the front of each sequin-covered shoe using the hot-glue gun. Leave the glue to dry fully.

✴ Slip on your sequin shoes, click your heels together, and see where you end up!

"**D**orothy said, with hesitation…
'I have not killed anything.'
'Your house did, anyway,' replied
the little old woman, with a laugh, 'and that is
the same thing. See!' She continued, pointing to
the corner of the house. 'There are her two feet,
still sticking out from under a block of wood.'
Dorothy looked and gave a little cry of fright.
There indeed, just under the corner of the great
beam the house rested on, two feet were sticking
out, shod in silver shoes with pointed toes."

~ Chapter 2 ~
The Council with the Munchkins

GLINDA DOLL

★ ★

Create your very own glamorous Good Witch from a simple wooden clothespin.

YOU WILL NEED

- Old-fashioned round wooden "dolly" clothespin with a split end
- 6" length of thick garden wire
- Hot-glue gun
- Red and black felt-tip pens for face
- 8"-wide-x-4³/₄"-long piece of pink cotton fabric
- 4" x 6" of silver tulle with glitter dots
- Two 2¹/₂"-x-6" pieces of white tulle
- Pink embroidery thread
- Thin orange yarn for hair
- Thin silver cardboard for crown
- Three silver star gems
- One round silver gem
- 2¹/₂" length of thin silver wire for wand

★ To make the basic frame and arms, loop the thick garden wire around the "body" of the clothespin, just above the split. Add a dot of glue at the back to hold the wire in place.

★ To create Glinda's face, draw her features on the "head" using the pens. It is best to draw the face now; it is easier to replace the clothespin now if you are dissatisfied with the results.

★ To make the underskirt, fold the pink fabric in half widthwise. With the folded edge at her feet, fix one end of the fabric in place with a line of glue just under the wire arms. Wrap the fabric around the body and fix the other end neatly at the back with a line of glue on the overlapping sides (1).

★ Lay the piece of silver tulle over the pink fabric. Make small pleats in the tulle as you wrap it around. Secure in place by again applying a line of glue around the top edge.

★ To cover the arms, add a dot of glue to the end of the left-hand wire. Attach one end of the pink embroidery thread to the wire and wrap to form a small ball. Continue wrapping the wire all the way up the arm until you reach the body. Carry the thread over to the right-hand arm and repeat; finish with a dot of glue and a small ball at the end (2). To cover the bodice, wrap the body diagonally in both directions until covered.

★ To make the hair, glue one end of the orange yarn to the back of the head. Wrap around the head neatly until covered. Finish with a dot of glue to the back of the head (3).

★ To make the sleeves, fold the pieces of white tulle in half lengthwise. Pinch the ends together and glue. Place over the arms and glue on the underside to secure. Glue the round gem to the front of the bodice.

★ Using the template on page 129, cut a crown from the silver cardboard. Glue the ends together, add a star gem to the front, and place on the head. To make the wand, sandwich the thin wire between two star gems. Glue in place to one hand.

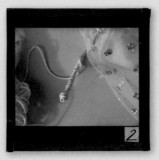

MUNCHKIN HAT EGG COZIES

✶ ✶

"The Munchkins wore round hats that rose to a small point a foot above their heads."
These decorated felt hats are cozy coverings for eggs!

YOU WILL NEED

- Selection of wool felt squares in various colors (we used three shades of blue, two shades of green, two shades of yellow, pink, and red)
- A selection of embroidery threads in contrasting colors
- Embroidery needle
- Scissors or pinking shears
- Selection of small felt pom-poms, buttons, sequins, and bells in various colors for decoration

To make the hat cozy

✶ Using the template on page 129, cut one hat from colored felt. Using the same template, cut one brim from a contrasting shade of felt. Place the brim in position on top of the hat and join the two pieces along the base using blanket stitch (1).

✶ With the brim on the inside, fold the hat in half lengthwise. Join the edges from bottom to top using blanket stitch. Turn about ¾" of the brim to the right side. This creates the basic hat.

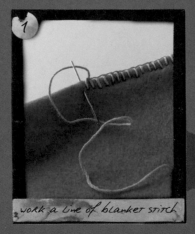

work a line of blanket stitch

To make the feather and flower decoration

✶ Using the templates on page 129, cut out different size feathers from colored felt and one flower center in a contrasting shade. For a crimped edge, use pinking shears to cut out the shapes. Lay the smaller feathers on top of the larger ones and sew in place with a line of running stitch. Tuck the tip of the feathers into the brim of the hat, then place the flower center on top and stitch in place (2). Add a few colored sequins to the center for decoration.

✶ Using the templates on page 129, cut two flower petals from colored felt; cut one center and one leaf in contrasting shades. Place one petal shape on top of the other to form a cross. Pinch together in the middle and secure with a few stitches. Add the center and leaf, then add a bell or button.

decorate with feathers

MUNCHKIN PLACE CARDS

"DOROTHY NOTICED A GROUP OF THE QUEEREST PEOPLE SHE HAD EVER SEEN. THEY WERE NOT AS BIG AS THE GROWN FOLK SHE HAD ALWAYS BEEN USED TO; BUT NEITHER WERE THEY VERY SMALL."

~ Chapter 2 ~
The Council with the Munchkins

We all know the Munchkins host great parties, so why not let them guide your guests to their seats?

YOU WILL NEED

- Two letter-size sheets of scrapbook paper in different patterns
- Spray glue
- 2" x 4" of thin white cardboard
- Black and pink felt-tip pens
- 4" x 4" of scrapbook paper in a contrasting pattern for girl's apron
- ¾" x 4" of thin glitter cardboard for boy's waistband
- Flower shapes punched from thin cardboard (optional)
- Small felt pom-poms
- Two 6" lengths of thin silver wire
- White craft glue
- Stapler
- Hot-glue gun

Makes 2 place cards

☆ Using spray glue, glue together the sheets of scrapbook paper so the patterned sides are face out. Using the templates on page 129, cut one body from the double-sided paper and cut one face from the white cardboard. Using felt-tip pens, draw features on the white cardboard face; it's fun to mimic the features of your guests (1).

☆ Glue the face in place on the body. Using a black felt-tip pen, add more details to the body, such as a collar, hair, and buttons on the hat. Using the templates on page 129, cut one apron for a girl or one waistband for a boy from a contrasting pattern. Glue in place on the body. Add a felt pom-pom to the hat and a punched paper flower to the apron (2).

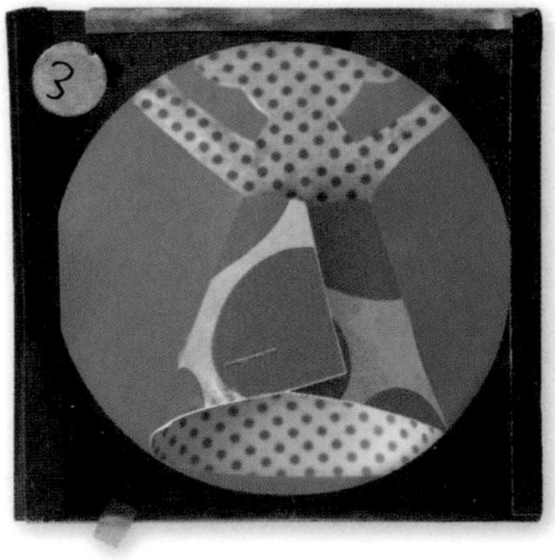

☆ Shape the skirt of the body into a cone by bending the corners back until they overlap by ⅜". Secure in place with a staple (3).

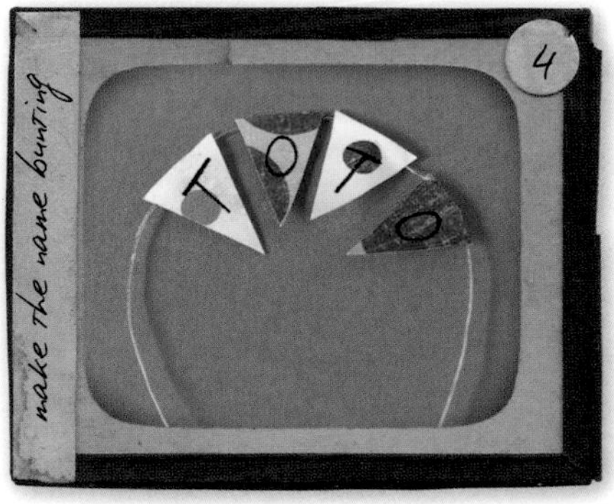

☆ Cut a paper triangle for each letter, write on the letters then attach to the wire using a hot-glue gun (4). Bend and cut the wire to size. Glue each end to the back of a hand.

Baum's Bazaar

❧ BOX O' BRICKS ❧
COCONUT ICE

This Yellow Brick Road coconut ice recipe will have you addicted to eating bricks!

YOU WILL NEED

- 13 ounces desiccated coconut
- 3 1/2 cups powdered sugar, sifted, plus extra for dusting
- 4 ounces condensed milk
- Few drops of vanilla extract
- Brown and yellow food coloring

Makes 12 bricks

✺ Place the desiccated coconut and powdered sugar together in a large mixing bowl. Add the condensed milk, a splash at a time, and combine until the mixture forms a dough but is not too wet.

✺ Place one-fifth of this mixture in a separate bowl and add a few drops of brown food coloring. To the other four-fifths of the mixture add yellow food coloring to create a vibrant shade.

✺ Lay three lengths of parchment paper on your work surface and dust with powdered sugar. Divide the yellow mixture into two halves. Place one half on a length of parchment paper and, using a rolling pin, roll out to a thickness of about 3/8", keeping the shape as square as possible. Repeat with the second half, then roll out the brown mixture to a thickness of about 1/8".

✺ Place the brown square, parchment side up, on top of one of the yellow squares. Using a rolling pin, lightly press down on the layers so they stick together, then peel away the parchment. Repeat with the remaining yellow square to create a sandwich with the brown layer in the middle. Take care when rolling not to flatten the layers of the block too much.

✺ Wrap the block in parchment paper, slide onto a baking sheet, and chill in the refrigerator to harden. Using a sharp knife, cut the block into individual brick shapes, each 3/4" x 1 1/2". For perfectly straight lines, use a metal ruler to cut the bricks.

"'The road to the City of Emeralds is paved with yellow brick,' said the Witch, 'so you cannot miss it.'"

~ Chapter 2 ~
The Council with the Munchkins

The No-Brainer SCARECROW

★ ★

Create your own supercute scarecrow. What he may lack in scariness, he makes up for in homespun charm!

YOU WILL NEED

- Two bamboo canes, one shorter than the other for the arms (adjust the length of the canes according to how tall you want your scarecrow to be, 5ft to 6ft)
- Brown garden twine
- Waterproof toy stuffing or straw for head and body
- Brown parcel tape
- 16" x 16" of burlap or similar rough brown fabric
- 1 yard of cotton print fabric for body
- 8" x 8" of white cotton fabric for collar
- Blue embroidery thread
- Three self-cover buttons molds
- Matching sewing thread
- Skein of yarn for hair

★ To make the frame, form a cross with the bamboo canes. The horizontal cane for the arms should be positioned about 8" from the top of the vertical cane. Make sure both arms are of equal length. Tie the canes together firmly using brown garden twine.

cover the head

★ To make the head, shape the toy stuffing or straw into a ball. Tape this ball to the top of the vertical cane. Don't worry if this looks messy—it will be covered in the next stage. Lay the head on one corner of the brown burlap fabric (1). Fold the other corners of the fabric over so it covers the head and tie securely around the neck with twine.

★ Using the template from page 130, enlarged to suit the size of your scarecrow, cut two body pieces from the cotton print fabric. Embroider a trouser fly outline on one body piece using blue thread. Cut one collar from the white cotton fabric and stitch to the same body piece at the neck edge.

★ Place the body pieces with right sides together. Sew, leaving the bottom edge open. Turn right side out. Place over the canes, sliding the horizontal cane from side to side.

★ Tuck the burlap into the body and stitch around the neck edge. Fill with toy stuffing or straw then close the bottom edge with blanket stitch (2). Cover the buttons with print fabric following the manufacturer's instructions and sew to the front of the body.

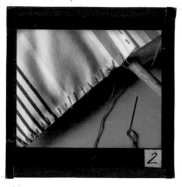

★ To make the hair, tightly wrap a 1¹⁄₄"-x-8" scrap of print fabric around the center of the skein of yarn and stitch in place on the top of the head. To finish, embroider or paint the scarecrow's face on the front of the head.

"THERE WAS A GREAT
CORNFIELD BEYOND THE
FENCE, AND NOT FAR AWAY
SHE SAW A SCARECROW, PLACED
HIGH ON A POLE TO KEEP
THE BIRDS AWAY FROM
THE RIPE CORN."

~ Chapter 3 ~
How Dorothy Saved the Scarecrow

RAFFIA FLOWER BASKET

★ ★ ★ ★ ★ ★ ★ ★ ★ ★ ★ ★ ★ ★ ★ ★ ★ ★ ★ ★

Customize a basket bag with these great lining and raffia flower techniques.

YOU WILL NEED

- Basket with handles

For the basket lining
- Lining fabric (to calculate how much you need, measure the basket following the instructions)
- Tape measure
- Matching sewing thread

For the decoration
- Lengths of raffia in two different colors
- Flower loom
- Blunt-ended tapestry needle
- Hot-glue gun
- Selection of wool felt in various colors

To make the basket lining

✶ First, measure the basket. To find the length of the side panels, measure from $2^1/2$" below the outside rim of the basket to the inside base. To find the width of the side panels, measure along the inside of one short and one long side of the basket. Measure the width and length of the inside of the basket's base. Add $1^1/4$" to all measurements for the seam allowances.

✶ Following these measurements, cut two side panels and one base panel from the lining fabric. Measure the position of the handles in relation to the rim. Transfer these measurements onto the side panels.

✶ Allowing for $5/8$" hems, cut triangular flaps at the marked points on the side panels to accommodate the handles. Turn under $5/8$" hems around these openings, notch the allowances and topstitch.

✶ Place the two side panels with right sides together. Stitch with $5/8$" seam allowances to form a tube. Pin the base panel to the sides, with right sides together (1). Stitch with a $5/8$" seam allowance, notching the seam if necessary.

✶ To make the ties, measure the outer rim of the basket. Divide this measurement in half, then add 16". Cut two $1^1/4$"-wide strips of lining fabric to this length. Fold the strips in half lengthwise, with right sides together, and press. Stitch along all sides.

✶ Turn under and press a $5/8$" hem all the way around the top edge of the lining. Leaving the end 8" free, pin then stitch the ties along the top edge, beginning and ending at the handle openings (2).

✶ Place the lining inside the basket and turn the overhanging lining down over the rim to the outer side of the basket. Knot the ties into decorative bows just below the handles.

attaching the lining base

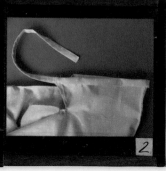

RAFFIA FLOWERS

This retro 1970s technique is a great way to vamp up any boring old bags, hats, or purses.

✳ Separate a length of raffia in your chosen color and tie a knot in it about 4" from one end. Thread the raffia through the hole at the edge of the flower loom. Check it is secure.

✳ Wind the raffia backward and forward over opposite pegs, traveling around the loom. You may need to join additional lengths of raffia onto the original piece; to do this simply tie the two ends into a neat knot and trim any excess. Once the raffia has been wound around all the pegs, trim the loose end to about 4" and knot to the first knotted end.

✳ Thread a tapestry needle with a different color raffia. Bring the needle up from the underside between the loops of one petal, then pass it back through the center of the flower. Repeat this until all the petals have been sewn.

✳ Once all the petals have been secured, carefully remove the raffia flower from the loom. Make as many raffia flowers in various sizes and colors as preferred.

✳ Using a hot-glue gun, attach the raffia flowers to the side of your basket. We also added extra felt flowers (see the instructions on page 22) and leaves, as well as pearl bead and bell trims.

Baum's Bazaar

DOROTHY
❧ GIFT TAGS ❧

for perfect presents and gorgeous gifts

.1.
COLOR-PHOTOCOPY
THE GIFT TAGS ONTO
THIN CARDBOARD.

.2.
CUT OUT THE GIFT
TAGS AND PUNCH
HOLES FOR THE
RIBBON TIES.

.3.
THREAD THE TAGS
WITH RIBBON
AND WRITE YOUR
MESSAGE ON
THE REVERSE.

The Scarecrow's
BRAN NEW BRAINS
MUFFINS

✫ ✫

*We all know the most important meal of the day is breakfast, so don't be a silly Scarecrow.
Why not have one of these delicious energy-fueled treats to keep your brains at their best!*

YOU WILL NEED

- ½ cup salted butter, room temperature
- ½ cup brown sugar
- 2 bananas, mashed
- ½ cup milk
- 1 teaspoon of vanilla extract
- 2 extra-large eggs, lightly beaten
- ¾ cup whole-wheat flour
- 4 ounces wheat bran
- 1 teaspoon baking powder
- 1 teaspoon baking soda
- ½ teaspoon salt
- 3 ounces chunky mixed nuts and granola breakfast cereal, plus extra for topping

✫ Preheat the oven to 375°F. Line a 6-hole or 12-hole muffin pan with paper cases following the instructions given below for Tulip Muffin Cases.

✫ Place the butter and sugar in a bowl and cream together until light and fluffy.

✫ Add the mashed bananas, milk, vanilla extract, and beaten eggs. Stir through until the ingredients are fully combined.

✫ In a separate bowl, combine the whole-wheat flour, wheat bran, baking powder and soda, and salt. Add the banana mixture. Once the ingredients are evenly mixed, gently stir in the breakfast cereal.

✫ Spoon the mixture into the tulip muffin cases and bake for 15 minutes. Remove from the oven and sprinkle with some extra cereal. Return to the oven and bake for 5–10 minutes more, or until a wooden skewer inserted into the middle of the muffins comes out clean.

✫ Leave to cool slightly in the muffin pan but serve while still warm, if you can.

make the muffin cases

TULIP MUFFIN CASES

YOU WILL NEED

- Muffin pan
- Unbleached parchment paper
- Paper cup
- Brown parcel string (optional)

✫ Cut the parchment paper into 6" squares, one for each muffin case required.

✫ Lay each square centrally over a muffin-pan hole and, using a paper cup, push the paper down into the hole to form a tulip shape. With your nails, score along the folds to define the natural creases in the paper.

✫ Add the muffin mixture to the cases and bake in the pan. Often the cases hold their shape better when doubled up.

✫ Once the muffins are cool, tie with a little brown string bow for a more rustic finish.

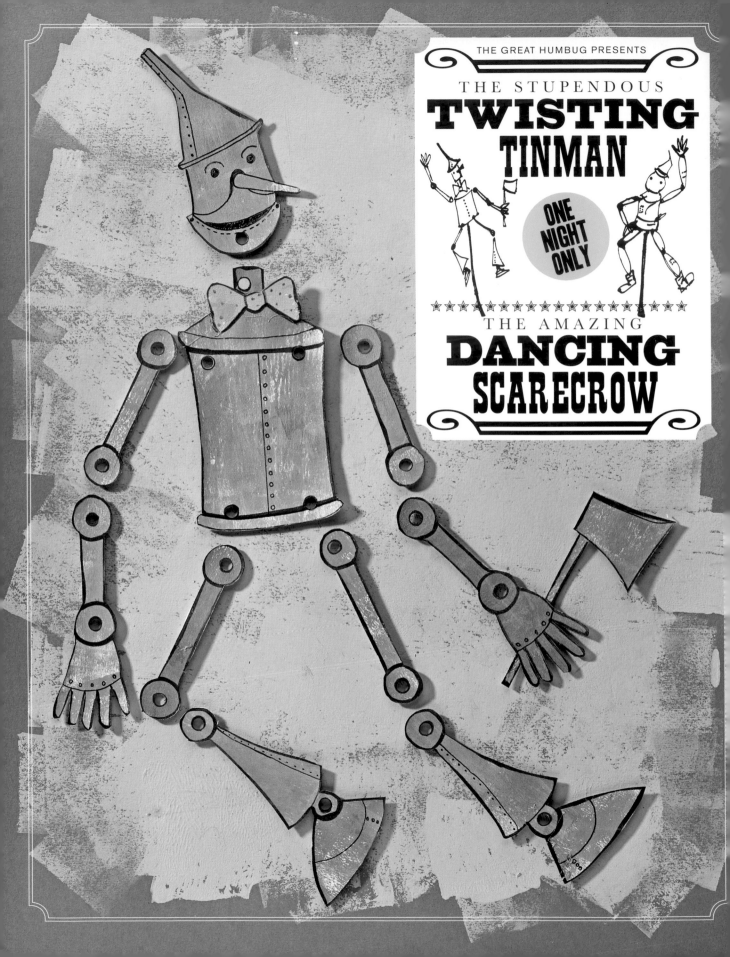

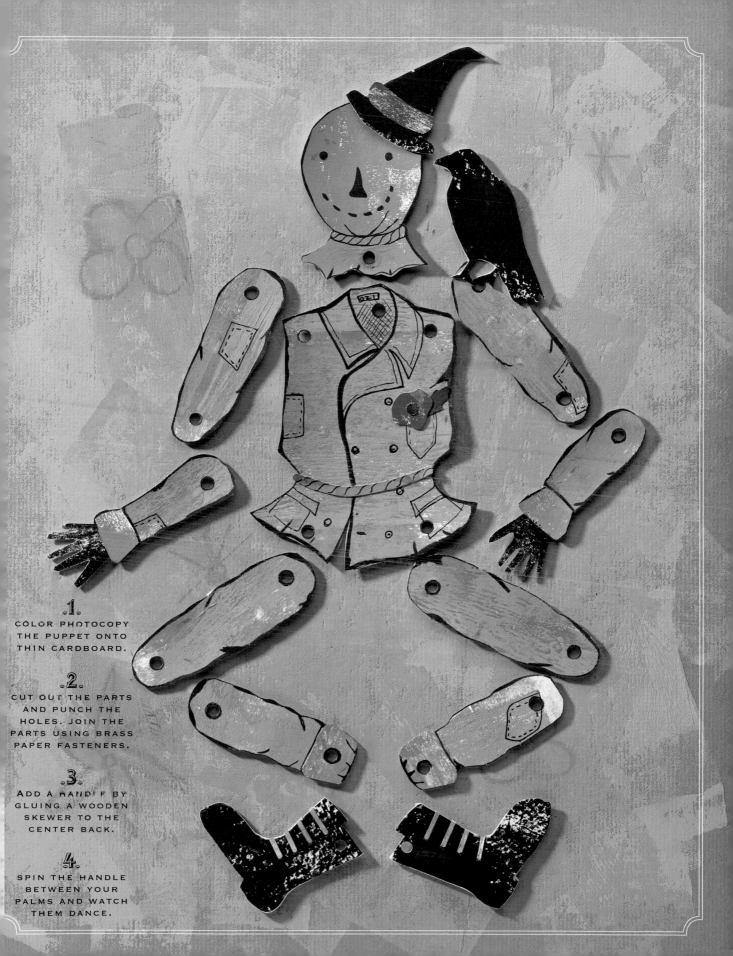

.1.
COLOR PHOTOCOPY
THE PUPPET ONTO
THIN CARDBOARD.

.2.
CUT OUT THE PARTS
AND PUNCH THE
HOLES. JOIN THE
PARTS USING BRASS
PAPER FASTENERS.

.3.
ADD A HANDLE BY
GLUING A WOODEN
SKEWER TO THE
CENTER BACK.

.4.
SPIN THE HANDLE
BETWEEN YOUR
PALMS AND WATCH
THEM DANCE.

The Tin Woodman's
HEART GARLAND

✶ ✶

All the Tin Woodman wanted was a heart, and with this garland he can have one for every day of the week.

YOU WILL NEED

- Tin or aluminum sheets, 1/64" thick
- Protective gloves
- Tin snips or old scissors
- Block of wood, for drilling and hammering
- Tin punch and hammer
- Wet-and-dry paper
- Electric drill
- Natural garden twine
- Small metal buttons
- Soft cloth
- Strong adhesive suitable for metals
- Small hammer

✶ Photocopy or trace the templates on page 131. Cut out each shape. Using a sharp pencil, draw around each paper template onto the tin sheets. For our garland, we made two large, three medium, and two small hearts plus two birds and two wings.

✶ Wearing protective gloves, cut out the shapes with the tin snips or scissors.

✶ Decide on your design for the decoration and draw it on the tin shapes with a pencil. Place the first heart on the wooden block then, using a small tin punch and hammer, tap out the design. Experiment with different size punches: for example, a flat-head screwdriver gives a rectangular shape. Also, the harder you hammer, the deeper the impression.

✶ To remove any sharp edges, dampen the wet-and-dry paper and rub all over the metal shapes in a circular motion. This burnishes the tin and makes the hammered pattern stand out.

✶ Drill hanging holes in the hearts and two larger holes at points A and B on the birds' backs. Use the wooden block for drilling.

✶ To make the garland, cut three 2¼-yard lengths of natural garden twine and braid together. Knot each end, leaving about 8" unbraided.

✶ Thread a tin bird onto each end of the braided garland. Using strong adhesive, glue the bird's wing in place so it covers the string and any holes. Glue a small button on top of the wing.

✶ To hang each heart, cut an 8" length of twine and fold in two. Thread both ends through the tin heart until only a small loop is left. Thread the two cut ends of twine through the loop. Repeat with the remaining hearts.

✶ Finally, hang the hearts, evenly spaced and according to size, along the braided garland in your preferred order.

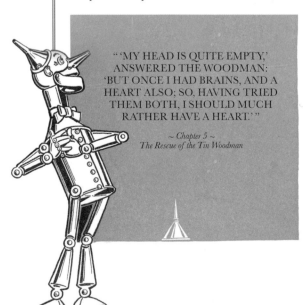

" 'MY HEAD IS QUITE EMPTY,' ANSWERED THE WOODMAN: 'BUT ONCE I HAD BRAINS, AND A HEART ALSO; SO, HAVING TRIED THEM BOTH, I SHOULD MUCH RATHER HAVE A HEART.' "

~ Chapter 5 ~
The Rescue of the Tin Woodman

TIN CAN LANTERNS

★ ★

Set the mood with these delectable votive-candle holders.

YOU WILL NEED

- Selection of tin cans, emptied, cleaned, and labels removed
- Marker pen
- Acrylic or spray paint in a selection of bright colors
- Wooden block (small enough to fit inside the empty cans)
- Electric drill
- Dustpan and brush

Caution: Never leave a lighted candle unattended.

★ Check that the tin cans are thoroughly clean; there must be no food residue on the inside or glue from the label on the outside.

★ Decide on your designs for the decoration and draw it on the outside of the cans with a marker pen.

★ Paint the inside of the cans a bright color. (Vibrant shades look great when illuminated by the candlelight.) Leave the paint to dry completely.

★ Place the wooden block inside the can; this makes it easier and safer when drilling the design. (If you don't have a wooden block, fill the can with water and freeze it.)

★ Following your design, drill small holes in the cans to create the decorative pattern. Once complete, brush away any tin residue and check for sharp edges.

★ Place a lighted votive candle inside each tin can lantern.

" 'I SHALL TAKE THE HEART,'
RETURNED THE WOODMAN,
'FOR BRAINS DO NOT MAKE ONE
HAPPY, AND HAPPINESS IS THE
BEST THING IN THE WORLD.' "

~ Chapter 5 ~
The Rescue of the Tin Woodman

CHOCOLATE "OIL" AND SILVER-NUT SUNDAE

This delicious warm chocolate sauce will keep your elbow joints moving—moving the spoon from the glass to your mouth!

YOU WILL NEED

For the chocolate sauce
- 4 ounces plain chocolate (minimum 70% cocoa solids)
- 14-ounce can sweetened condensed milk
- 2 tablespoons butter
- 1 teaspoon vanilla extract

For the silver nuts
- Few handfuls of mixed nuts, such as almonds, hazelnuts, and walnuts
- Edible silver paint spray

For the sundae
- Vanilla ice cream
- Edible silver stars and chocolate stars for decoration
- Indoor sparklers (optional)

Makes 4 sundaes

For the chocolate sauce

☆ Break the chocolate into chunks and place half of it into a heavy-bottom saucepan.

☆ Add the condensed milk and butter then place over medium heat. Stir continuously until the chocolate has melted—do not allow the mixture to boil.

☆ Check the sauce and—if you want an even more chocolaty taste—add more squares of chocolate. (This isn't strictly necessary as you can simply add all the chocolate at the beginning, but any excuse to try the sauce!)

☆ Remove the sauce from the heat and stir in the vanilla extract.

For the silver nuts

☆ Place the mixed nuts in a dry frying pan and toast for a couple of minutes over a high heat. Leave to cool.

☆ Once cool, spray the nuts with edible silver paint spray. Leave to dry completely.

To assemble the sundae

☆ Place a few of the silver nuts in the bottom of a sundae glass. Pour over a glug of the warm chocolate sauce then add a scoop of vanilla ice cream. Repeat this to create another layer. Top the sundae with two round scoops of vanilla ice cream then drizzle over some more warm chocolate sauce. Decorate with a few more silver nuts, a chocolate star, and a sprinkle of edible silver stars.

The Cowardly Lion
HAND PUPPET

★ ★

This little lion with his shivering, quivering mane isn't scared of a thing, no Siree, not him, no way. "Ooh, what was that?"

YOU WILL NEED

- Four pieces, each 9" x 12", of yellow wool felt for face and body
- 9" x 12" of orange wool felt for mane
- 9" x 12" of cream wool felt for muzzle
- 9" x 12" of pink wool felt for ears, nose, and mouth
- Various scraps of print fabrics for tummy and mane, maximum size 8" x 16"
- Embroidery thread in each of the following colors: yellow, orange, pink, and black
- Two $3/8$"– $5/8$" black buttons for eyes
- Scissors
- Felt flower in a contrasting color (optional)

baste the ears in place

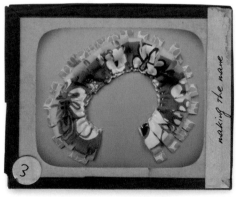
making the mane

stitch mane in place

★ Using the templates on pages 132–33, cut all the required pieces from colored felt and print fabric. Sew the tummy onto the front body. Add the paw detail to two of the arms and sew them together in pairs (1).

★ Sew the pink inner ears to the orange outer ears then position the ears either side of the face and baste in place (2).

★ For the mane, cut three rectangles—one 4" x 16" from orange felt, one $3^{1}/4$" x 16" and one $5^{1}/2$" x 16" from print fabrics. Fold each rectangle in half lengthwise and place in a

stack with the felt in the middle. Join the layers along the raw edges with running stitches, then slightly gather. Make $1^{1}/4$" snips into each layer of the mane at $3/4$" intervals along the folded edge (3). Position the mane around the top in the back and baste in place. Place the face on top and stitch (4).

✳ Fold the pink mouth in half along
the dotted line. Sew a line of running
stitch just inside the folded edge (5).
This prevents the mouth opening too
wide and getting stuck in a roar!

✳ Sew the bottom lip to the front body,
matching points A on the templates.
Then sew the top lip to the muzzle,
matching points B (6). Sew the top of
the muzzle to the face, matching points
C, but with the muzzle overlapping the
face by ³⁄₈". Insert the arms in between
the front and back body pieces at about
1¹⁄₄" down from the corners of the
mouth. Sew the side edges together.
The front is longer than the back at the
base of the puppet.

✳ Stitch or glue the pink nose to the
muzzle and embroider on a set of
whiskers using pink and black
embroidery threads. Sew the buttons
to the face just above the muzzle for the
eyes. Alternatively, use felt shapes,
beads, or teddy bear eyes.

✳ Make a small fringe from print
fabric in the same way as the mane and
stitch in between the ears. For extra

VISIT THE Emerald City

JUST FOLLOW THE YELLOW BRICK ROAD

GIANT ROSETTES

Awarded for COURAGE

✦✦✦✦✦✦✦✦✦✦✦✦✦✦✦✦✦✦✦✦✦✦✦✦✦✦✦✦✦

Sometimes decorating a party can seem daunting, but take courage! Why not take a leaf out of the Lion's book by creating these stunningly simple rosettes?

YOU WILL NEED

- Three large sheets of paper, each 22" x 34", in contrasting colors for each rosette
- Two letter-size sheets of patterned scrapbook paper for rosette center and ribbons for each rosette
- Thin silver wire
- Stapler
- Glue
- Length of ribbon for hanging

✭ First, decide on your color scheme and the order in which they will be placed. The entire width of a large sheet of paper is used for the base rosette ring, then different colored rings are added to build the design.

✭ Lay the three large sheets of paper one on top of the other, and concertina fold them widthwise into a fan shape by folding backward and forward in 2¹/₄" widths. Use the edge of a metal ruler to make crisp folds.

concertina the papers together

✭ Once the papers are fully folded, open out the concertina and separate the sheets. Trim both ends of each sheet into a gently curved petal shape.

✭ Cut the second sheet about 4" shorter either side than the first, so the middle rosette ring will have space around it. Repeat for the third sheet but 8" shorter.

✭ Layer the sheets together again, matching the folds exactly and making sure the smallest piece is centrally placed (1).

✭ With the papers lined up, fold the fan in half to find the center point. Wrap the wire around the center point in a loop, tightly securing the sheets. Open out the rosette and staple each end together to join.

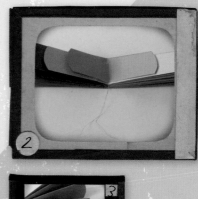

✭ From patterned scrapbook paper, cut a circle to your preferred size and glue to the center of the rosette. Add two paper ribbon lengths, glued to the reverse of the rosette.

✭ Attach a length of ribbon to the wired center and hang at your desired location.

"There were big yellow and white and blue and purple blossoms, besides great clusters of scarlet poppies, which were so brilliant in color they almost dazzled Dorothy's eyes."

~ Chapter 8 ~
The Deadly Poppy Field

FIELD O' POPPIES

★ ★

These stunning giant flowers look fantastic in bunches and can be made any size.
They are great to use big as party decorations, or make in a smaller display for a table.

YOU WILL NEED

- 8½" x 11" of thin red cardboard
- 11" x 17" of thin black and leaf green cardboard
- 1-yard-long bamboo cane
- Green spray paint (same color as leaf green cardboard)
- Duct tape
- Red glitter

concertina fold the petals

shape the petals

★ Using the templates on page 134, for each poppy cut out five petals from red cardboard, two stamens from black, and two leaves from green.

★ Concertina fold the petals lengthwise about three-quarters of the way up. Make sure the center fold is in line with the slit and is a valley fold—in other words, it folds inward (1).

★ Flatten the petal folds out slightly. To curve the petal, overlap the base of the petal where there is a slit and staple in place (2). Repeat for all the petals.

★ Staple three petals together in a rough triangle, with two close together and the third slightly on its own (3).

add the final poppy petals

4

★ Place the remaining two petals either side of the single petal. Staple in place (4).

5

create the stamen

★ Fold the stalks of the stamen in toward the center. Place the two stamens together with the stalks misaligned and glue in the center (5). Gently curl the stamen stalk ends using either the blades of a closed pair of scissors or your fingers.

6

unfurl the finished flower

★ Glue the stamens in the center of the poppy. Unfurl each poppy petal and gently curl outward at the top (6).

★ Spray the bamboo cane with green paint and leave to dry. Score the green leaves down the center and, using a hot-glue gun, glue them to the cane.

★ To attach the poppy head to the stem, use strips of duct tape. Cut four strips of tape. Stick the first three strips along the underside of the poppy head down onto the bamboo cane. Wrap the final strip of tape around the other three to secure the flower. Try to do this as neatly as possible.

★ For a magical finish, sprinkle the poppies with red glitter sleepy dust.

Raggedy Patchwork
POPPY T-SHIRT
✶✶✶✶✶✶✶✶✶✶✶✶✶✶✶✶✶✶✶✶✶✶✶✶✶✶✶✶✶✶

Be truly en vogue with this beautiful poppy-embellished T-shirt. Adding poppies is a great way to customize clothes that need a new lease on life.

✰ Cut sets of four circles all the same size from the different fabrics (1). To vary the flower sizes, cut some sets in varying sizes from one another, making some very small and others oversized.

✰ Lay the circles on top of one another and fold in half, then into quarters (2). Pinching the tip, stitch across the bottom edges to secure the shape (3). Repeat for as many poppies as you require.

✰ Lay the poppies on your T-shirt before you attach them and pin into place. Once happy with the design, stitch neatly from below at the point of the flower and either side of the bottom petal layer (4).

pinch the petals together

sew onto the t-shirt

SLEEPY-TIME EYEMASK

✦✦✦✦✦✦✦✦✦✦✦✦✦✦✦✦✦✦✦✦✦✦✦✦✦✦✦✦✦✦✦✦

*When you're in need of forty winks, this embroidered eyemask
will help you drift off into a field of dreams.*

- 20" x 20" of pale blue silk fabric for eyemask front
- Dressmaker's disappearing-ink pen
- Embroidery hoop, at least 10" in diameter
- Embroidery floss in various colors
- Metallic embroidery threads
- Fine embroidery needle
- 10" x 10" of mid-blue silk fabric for eyemask back
- 10" x 10" of soft fabric, such as velour or flannelette, for padding
- 2" x 20" of pale blue silk fabric for eyemask strap
- 12" length of $1/4$"-wide elastic (adjust the length of the elastic to suit your head size)
- Narrow midnight blue ribbon (optional)

To stitch the embroidery

✳ Trace the design on page 135 onto the center of the large piece of pale blue silk with a disappearing-ink pen. It is easier to see the lines if you hold the fabric up against a window. Mount the silk in an embroidery hoop, making sure the fabric is taut. Using two strands of embroidery floss and a fine needle, embroider the poppies by working small neat stitches over the guidelines (1).

embroider the poppy design

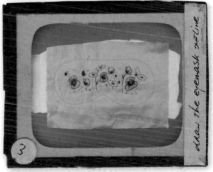

draw the eyemask outline

To make the eyemask front

✳ Remove the embroidery from the hoop and lightly press. Using the template on page 135, trace the outline of the eyemask onto the silk, making sure the poppies sit across the center. Lay the embroidered silk right side up on top of the padding. Pin the layers together then stitch all the way around, $3/8$" outside the outline (3). Cut out the eyemask front close to this stitching line.

To make the strap

✳ Fold the narrow piece of pale blue silk in half lengthwise. Stitch down the long edge, about $5/8$" in from the fold. Silk frays, so keep a slightly wider than normal seam allowance. Turn right side out and press with the seam in the center of one side of this tube. Thread the elastic through the tube and fix to one end of the strap, securing it with a few stitches. Gather the silk tube evenly along its length and secure the other end of the elastic to the strap, again with a few stitches.

☆ Pin the layers together. Leaving a 2"–2½" opening along the straight top edge and avoiding the strap, stitch all the way around the eyemask following the template line.

☆ Trim the seam allowance back to about ¼"; it's fine to trim away the first stitching line from the eyemask front. Around the curves, snip small notches from the seam allowance to allow the fabric to stretch. Turn the eyemask right side out through the opening. The strap will fall in place at the back of the eyemask. Gently ease the curves into shape and lightly press. Close the opening with small neat hand stitches. Tie short lengths of midnight blue ribbon in neat bows at each end of the strap, if preferred.

☆ Baste the elasticized strap to the embroidered eyemask front at points A and B. Place the eyemask front on the mid-blue silk, with right sides together. Arrange the strap so that it is contained within the shape of the eyemask front except the center section, which should be visible at the top of the eyemask (4).

"They now came upon more and more of the big scarlet poppies, and fewer and fewer of the other flowers; and soon they found themselves in the midst of a great meadow of poppies. Now it is well known that when there are many of these flowers together their odor is so powerful that anyone who breathes it falls asleep, and if the sleeper is not carried away from the scent of the flowers, he sleeps on and on forever. But Dorothy did not know this, nor could she get away from the bright red flowers that were everywhere about; so presently her eyes grew heavy and she felt she must sit down to rest and to sleep."

~ Chapter 8 ~
The Deadly Poppy Field

OVER THE RAINBOW CAKE

✶ ✶

This cake is the perfect centerpiece to any party; make this for someone's birthday and take great delight in seeing the surprise on her face when she cuts the first slice!

YOU WILL NEED

For the cake

- 1½ cups unsalted butter, at room temperature
- 1½ cups superfine sugar
- 5 extra-large egg whites
- 3 teaspoons vanilla extract
- 2⅓ cups self-raising flour
- 3 teaspoons baking powder
- ¾ cup plus 2 tablespoons milk
- Violet, blue, green, yellow, orange, and red natural food coloring

For the frosting

- 1¾ cups cream cheese
- ⅓ cup plus 1 tablespoon unsalted butter, at room temperature
- 2⅓ cups powdered sugar
- 2 teaspoons lemon flavoring

For the decoration

- Soft candy diamonds

You will also need:
- A selection of mixing bowls
- Round 8" cake pans
- Wire cooling rack
- Cardboard cake mat
- Lazy Susan
- Plastic side-scraper

Serves 8–12 slices

To make the cake

✶ Preheat the oven to 350°F. Line the cake pans with parchment paper.

✶ Place the butter and sugar in a large bowl and cream together until light and fluffy. Whisk the egg whites into the butter, one by one. Add the vanilla extract.

✶ In a separate bowl, sift together the flour and baking powder. Gradually add the flour to the butter, stirring only until the batter is just combined. Finally add the milk.

✶ Divide the batter equally into six bowls for the different colored cake layers, with each sixth weighing about 9 ounces. Add a few drops of one of the natural food colors to each bowl, blending the color evenly.

✶ Spoon one of the colored cake batters into a prepared cake pan and bake for 10–12 minutes, or until the top of the cake springs back to the touch. Ideally, use two or more cake pans and bake several layers together at the same time. Allow the cakes to cool fully before assembling and adding the frosting.

To make the frosting

✶ Place the cream cheese and butter in a bowl; blend until smooth. Sift in the powdered sugar and add the lemon flavoring.

To assemble the cake

✶ Place a cardboard cake mat on a lazy Susan. Lay the violet-colored cake layer on a sheet of parchment paper and place on the lazy Susan. Spread a thin coating of frosting evenly over the cake layer, then place the blue-colored cake on top. Repeat for each layer.

✶ To crumb coat the layered cake, spoon a generous amount of frosting on top of the cake (1). Using a side-scraper, spread it evenly across the top and down the sides, turning the lazy Susan against the direction of the side-scraper. Chill the cake for at least 30 minutes or until the frosting has set.

✶ For the final coat of frosting, repeat the previous stage with the remaining clean frosting. To finish, decorate the top of the cake with multicolored candy diamonds.

assemble the cake in layers

hey all started upon the Journey, greatly enjoying the walk through the soft, fresh grass; and it was not long before they reached the road of yellow brick and turned again toward the Emerald City where the great Oz dwelt."

~ Chapter 10 ~
The Guardian of the Gates

PATCHWORK PICNIC SET

✶ ✶

Small sitting pads are ideal for picnics—everyone gets their own seat and there are no fights for more space on the blanket. They even have a waterproof base for damp days.

YOU WILL NEED

For each sitting pad

- 9" x 9" of solid-colored cotton for center square
- Selection of quilting prints, maximum 12" x 20"
- Fusible adhesive web
- Matching sewing threads
- Thick cardboard and ruler
- Quilter's rotary cutter and cutting mat
- 20" x 20" of white lining fabric
- $2^1/2$" x $13^3/4$" each of waterproof-coated fabric and quilting cotton for handle
- 20" x 20" of waterproof-coated fabric for backing
- 19" x 19" of batting, $^3/4$" thick

For the tablecloth

- $12^1/2$" x $24^1/4$" of print fabric, in three different colors
- $12^1/2$" x $35^1/2$" of print fabric, in two different colors
- $8^1/4$" x $11^1/2$" of cotton in four different solid colors for "place mats"
- 4" x 4" of cotton in four different prints for "coasters"
- $35^1/2$" x $47^1/4$" of cotton for backing

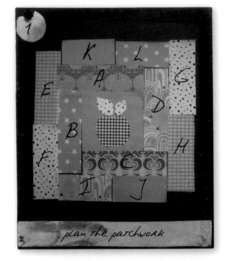

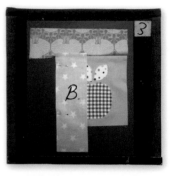

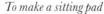
plan the patchwork

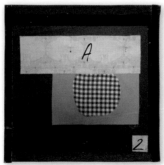

To make a sitting pad

✶ Using the templates on page 136, trace a reversed outline of the apple, heart, dog, or house motifs onto the paper side of the fusible adhesive web. Cut it out roughly and, with the adhesive side downward, iron to the wrong side of the chosen print fabric. Next, trim precisely around the traced outline, peel away the paper, and place the appliqué motif at the center of the plain center square. Press with a hot iron to fuse the adhesive.

✶ Secure the raw edges of the motif with either neat hand stitches or zigzag machine stitches in a colored thread.

✶ Measure and cut three rectangular templates from thick cardboard, one in each of the following sizes: $3^3/4$" x $11^3/4$" (pieces A–D), $3^3/4$" x $10^1/2$" (pieces E–H), $3^3/4$" x $7^3/4$" (pieces I–L).

✳ Select which prints you want for the patchwork rectangles, then press the fabric to remove any creases. Using the three cardboard templates, cut four rectangles of each size. For perfectly straight edges, use a quilter's rotary cutter and cutting mat.

✳ Lay out all your patchwork pieces and make a record of the plan (1). You will need to refer back to this plan as you sew the pieces together.

✳ With right sides together, place patchwork piece A on the center square, with raw edges aligned along the top edge. Machine stitch leaving a seam allowance of $1/2$"; stop at the edge of the center square, leaving about $3 1/4$" of the rectangle unstitched (2). Repeat with the remaining three pieces B, C, and D (3, 4, 5). When sewing on piece D, stitch along the entire length of the rectangle including the short side of piece A (5).

✳ Go back around the square and stitch the three unstitched ends of the rectangles to the short ends of the adjacent pieces. Press open the seams so they lie flat. Check that the outside edges of the resulting patchwork square are straight and, if any of them are a bit uneven, trim them square (6).

position the handle

★ Sew together pieces E and F along one short edge. Repeat with G and H, I and J, K and L. Press the seams open.

★ Sew the strip made from pieces I/J to the bottom edge of the patchwork square, aligning the seam of the strip with the middle of the center square. Repeat at the top edge with the strip made from pieces K/L.

★ Sew the longer strips made from pieces E/F and G/H to the left and right edges, again aligning the seams with the middle of the center square. Press open all the seams so they lie flat. Check that the outside edges of the final patchwork square are straight and, as before, trim if necessary.

★ Place the finished patchwork square on the lining, with wrong sides together. Leaving a 4" opening along one edge, stitch all the way around, leaving a $^1/_4$" seam allowance.

To make a handle
★ With right sides together, place the waterproof-fabric and cotton handle pieces together. Leaving an opening at one end, stitch all the way around to form a tube. Turn right side out and press. Fold the handle into a C-shape and pin centrally to the top edge of the patchwork square with the handle facing inward (7).

★ With right sides together, place the patchwork and oilcloth squares together. (The handle will be sandwiched between the two layers.) Starting at the bottom edge and leaving a 4" opening, stitch all the way around. Turn right side out and press.

★ Feed the square of batting through the opening, pushing into the corners

and flattening it out. If necessary, trim the batting for a snug fit.

★ Close the opening with small, neat hand stitches. You have now completed one sitting pad.

To make the tablecloth
★ With one $12^1/_2$"-x-$24^1/_4$" rectangle as the center panel, join the four other patchwork pieces to this panel in the same way as given for the pads. Press open all the seams so they lie flat.

★ Position the "place mats" and "coasters" on the patchwork tablecloth and stitch in place. Add appliqué motifs if preferred.

★ Place the patchwork tablecloth on the backing fabric, with right sides together. Leaving a 8" opening along one edge, stitch around the edge.

★ Turn the tablecloth right side out and press. Close the opening with small, neat hand stitches.

WELCOME TO THE EMERALD CITY

"BEFORE THEM STOOD A LITTLE
MAN ABOUT THE SAME SIZE
AS THE MUNCHKINS. HE WAS
CLOTHED ALL IN GREEN . . .

WHEN HE SAW DOROTHY AND
HER COMPANIONS THE MAN
ASKED, 'WHAT DO YOU WISH
IN THE EMERALD CITY?'
'WE CAME HERE TO SEE THE
GREAT OZ,' SAID DOROTHY.
THE MAN WAS SO SURPRISED
AT THIS ANSWER THAT HE
SAT DOWN TO THINK IT OVER."

~ Chapter 10 ~
The Guardian of the Gates

GLOW-IN-THE-DARK EMERALD CITY JELL-O

Dazzle your party guests with this marvelous Jell-O display and they will turn green with envy!

YOU WILL NEED Tonic water with quinine ★ Lime Jello-O mix UV light ★ Selection of plastic sandcastle molds

★ To make the Jell-O, follow the instructions from the green Jello-O packet, but in the final stage add the tonic water instead of water.

★ Using clean dry sandcastle molds you can form cityscapes. If your molds will not stand alone, put each one in a bowl and surround it with some paper towels to keep the molds steady. Pour your Jell-O liquid into the molds and leave to set in the refrigerator. The quinine in the Jell-O will pick up UV light and appear to glow; it also gives a distinctive bitter taste, which goes well with lime flavor.

★ Turn out your set Jell-O on a plate, turn down the lights, and hold up your UV light to show off the Emerald City's glow!

BAUM'S BAZAAR

At Baum's Bazaar you'll find by far, the finest goods in town,
The cheapest too as you'll find true, if you'll just step around

THE EMERALD CITY'S NO.1. DEPARTMENT STORE

-BASEMENT-	-FIRST FLOOR-	-SECOND FLOOR-
THE WORLD EMPORIUM	TAKE LUNCH & AFTERNOON TEA **MUNCHIES TEA LOUNGE** 12–4 DAILY	VISIT OUR NEW CONFECTIONERY CONCESSION
BEAUTIFUL GIFTS *China Teasets Direct from Quadling Co. & Other Exquisite Fare from All Over Oz*	MENU INCLUDES *Green Lipped Mussels Asparagus & Olive Pâté Apple & Pear Tart Greengage Jell-O*	DELECTABLE FARE *Emerald Iced Gem Cookies Pistachio Popcorn Green Lemonade Baum's Button Cookies*

BAUM'S BAZAAR
147–152 MINT BOULEVARD. EMERALD CITY. OZ

Baum's Bazaar
ICED GEM COOKIES

These old favorites are a bestseller on the Oz Candy Cart. As soon as they're in stock, they sell out!

YOU WILL NEED

- $1/2$ cup butter, softened
- $2/3$ cup superfine sugar
- 1 large egg, lightly beaten
- 2–3 drops vanilla extract
- $1 1/3$ cups plus 1 tablespoon all-purpose flour
- $1/4$ teaspoon baking powder
- $1/4$ teaspoon salt

For the icing
- 11 ounces royal icing sugar
- Green food coloring
- Edible green glitter

Makes about 30 cookies

✳ Place the butter and sugar in a large bowl and cream together until light and fluffy. Add the beaten egg and the vanilla extract.

✳ In a separate bowl, sift together the flour, baking powder, and salt. Gradually add the flour to the butter to form a dough.

✳ Wrap the dough in plastic wrap and chill in the refrigerator for at least 1 hour, but it can be left overnight.

✳ When ready to bake, preheat the oven to 400°F.

✳ Place the dough on a floured surface and roll out to about $1/4$" thick. Using a 2" round serrated cookie cutter, press out the shapes. Place on ungreased baking sheets about $3/4$" apart.

✳ Bake for 6–10 minutes until the cookies are golden brown at the edges. Leave to cool completely on a wire rack.

For the icing
✳ Sift the powdered sugar into a medium-sized bowl. Add a few drops of green food coloring and blend. Slowly add a little water—a drop at a time—to create a thick paste consistency.

✳ Using a $3/8$"-wide star tip, pipe the icing onto the centers of the cookies. For extra sparkly gems, sprinkle with green edible glitter.

Baum's Bazaar
PISTACHIO POPCORN

The citizens of Oz favor this delicious salty-sweet popcorn, but it is a little too spicy for the sugary-toothed Munchkins.

YOU WILL NEED

- 8 ounces pistachios, roasted, salted, and shelled
- 4 ounces plain popcorn
- 2 tablespoons unsalted butter
- 3 tablespoons maple syrup
- ½ teaspoon curry powder
- Green food coloring

☆ Pile the pistachios in the center of a clean tea towel and gather up the edges. Using a rolling pin, smash the pistachios into small pieces. Place the nuts in a large bowl and add the popcorn.

☆ Melt the butter in a small saucepan over a low heat. Add the maple syrup and curry powder, then simmer for 3 minutes. Add a few drops of food coloring and mix. Remove from the heat, pour the butter over the nuts and popcorn, then stir to coat.

☆ Leave to cool before serving or storing in an airtight container.

Baum's Bazaar

GREEN LEMONADE

The children of Oz simply love this green lemonade. It is rumored to be enjoyed by the Wizard himself, with ice and a dash of vodka on a hot day.

YOU WILL NEED
- 6 cups water
- 2 lemons & 4 limes
- 6 tablespoons superfine sugar (more for a sweeter drink)

✳ Place the water in a deep saucepan. Cut the two lemons and three of the limes in half, squeeze the juice and pips into the water and drop in the squeezed halves. Place over a high heat and bring to a boil (this can take 10 minutes).

✳ Reduce the heat, add the sugar, and simmer. Turn off the heat and leave the liquid to cool in the saucepan. As it cools, check the sweetness and add more sugar to taste.

✳ Once cool, strain the lemonade into a jug and chill.

✳ Serve with crushed ice and slices of the reserved lime. For an alcoholic cocktail, add vodka.

Baum's Bazaar
BAUM'S
❧ BUTTONS ❧

These dainty shortbread treats are a cute twist on the basic round cookie.

YOU WILL NEED

- ³/₄ cup butter, softened
- 1 cup superfine sugar
- 1 teaspoon vanilla extract
- 1¹/₃ cups all-purpose flour
- 4 ounces ground almonds (40 blanched almonds, finely ground)
- Green and blue food coloring

Makes about 50 cookies

To make two different shades of buttons
✶ Divide the ingredients in two before mixing, then color to different shades.

✶ Place the butter and sugar in a bowl and cream together until light and fluffy. Add a few drops of each food coloring and blend to the desired shade. Add the vanilla extract and mix well.

✶ In a separate bowl, sift the flour and add the ground almonds. Gradually add to the butter to form a dough. Wrap the dough in plastic wrap and chill for 2 hours.

✶ Preheat the oven to 325°F. On a floured surface, roll out the dough to a ¹/₄" thickness. Using a 2" round cookie cutter, press out the shapes. Place on ungreased baking sheets ³/₈" apart.

✶ To make the button rim, press a 1¹/₂" round jar lid into each cookie. To make the button holes, push a cylindrical lollypop stick into the center. Vary the number of holes between four and two. Bake in the oven for 6–10 minutes.

"GREEN CANDY AND GREEN POPCORN WERE OFFERED FOR SALE, AS WELL AS GREEN SHOES, GREEN HATS, AND GREEN CLOTHES OF ALL SORTS. AT ONE PLACE A MAN WAS SELLING GREEN LEMONADE, AND WHEN THE CHILDREN BOUGHT IT DOROTHY COULD SEE THAT THEY PAID FOR IT WITH GREEN PENNIES."

~ Chapter 11 ~
The Wonderful Emerald City of Oz

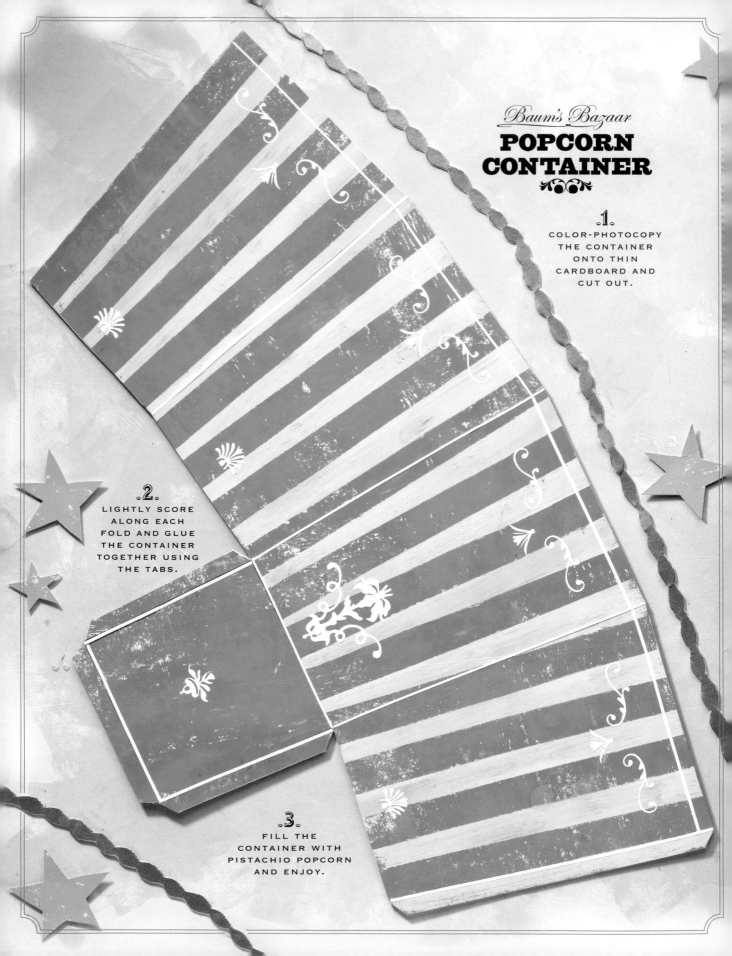

Baum's Bazaar

POPCORN CONTAINER

.1.
COLOR-PHOTOCOPY
THE CONTAINER
ONTO THIN
CARDBOARD AND
CUT OUT.

.2.
LIGHTLY SCORE
ALONG EACH
FOLD AND GLUE
THE CONTAINER
TOGETHER USING
THE TABS.

.3.
FILL THE
CONTAINER WITH
PISTACHIO POPCORN
AND ENJOY.

Baum's Bazaar

EMERALD GLASSES

.1.
COLOR-PHOTOCOPY
THE GLASSES ONTO
THIN CARDBOARD
AND CUT OUT.

.2.
GLUE THE ARMS TO
THE MAIN FRAME
AND FOLD AT THE
HINGES.

.3.
CUT OUT THE
STAR LENSES AND
REPLACE WITH
GREEN CANDY
WRAPPERS.

Extravagantly Embellished
EMERALD HAIRPIECES

✦ ✦

These emerald hairpieces are great for any occasion where you need a little extra sparkle in your life. The different styles are suitable for any hair type, just choose your favorite.

YOU WILL NEED

- 20" x 20" of sinamay mesh fabric (use brown for dark hair, beige for fair hair)
- 1 yard of gold cord
- A selection of bugle beads, seed beads, and other beads, gems, or stones that take your fancy (if the beads have holes they can be sewed on, if they don't then they must be glued on)
- Appliqué sequin star
- Wooden embroidery hoop
- Appliqué glue or any other glue that dries clear
- Hot glue-gun
- Pale-colored thread
- Needle
- Scissors
- Thin metal or fabric-covered hairband
- Haircomb

Sinamay is used by milliners in the making of hats and fascinators, so it provides a great base for these emerald hairpieces. Stretching the sinamay over an embroidery hoop keeps it taut and makes it easier to sew the beads in place. If you can't find sinamay, stiff cross-stitch fabric works just as well. The basic method given here can be used to create either hairpiece design.

To make the starburst hairpiece
✦ Using the template on page 136, trace the starburst shape onto paper and cut out. Mount the sinamay in the embroidery hoop and stretch taut.

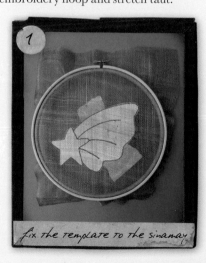

fix the template to the sinamay

✦ Tape the cutout template to the underside of the sinamay (1).

✦ Following the template, lay the gold cord on the sinamay and secure with small running stitches along the center. Sew or glue the appliqué sequin star in place. (You can make your own star from sequins, but using an appliqué patch saves time.)

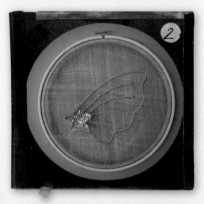

✦ Once the cord outline has been completed, gently remove the cutout template from the underside (2). Take care not to rip out any stitches.

✦ Starting at the narrow end nearest the star, lay out the largest beads within the cord outline. When you are happy with the design, make a note of the placement of all the beads. Remove the beads and, working one vertical row at at time, begin either sewing or gluing each one in place on the sinamay according to the plan.

attach the hairpiece to a hairband

fill the spaces with beads

★ Fill in the spaces between the larger beads or gems with small bugle or seed beads. It is quicker and neater to add three or four beads to the thread at a time, then stitch in place (3).

★ Once all the spaces have been filled, remove the sinamay from the embroidery hoop and carefully trim away the excess. Coat the reverse side of the design with a thin layer of appliqué glue or any other glue that dries clear; this keeps stray threads in place and strengthens the hairpiece.

★ Depending on where and how you plan to wear your hairpiece, either hot glue the sinamay onto a hairband or fix in your hair using hairpins (4).

To make the flower cluster hairpiece
★ Rather than using a template, this hairpiece was made freehand using teardrop-shaped gems to create each bloom. Stretch the sinamay taut over an embroidery hoop, as before. Using six large teardrop-shape stones, make the center flower. Sew a sequin in the middle and outline with bugle beads. Using smaller stones, make two flowers on either side and outline with seed beads. Trim the sinamay and coat with a layer of glue. Hot glue the beaded flowers to the upper bar of the haircomb (5).

DECORATED DOGHOUSE

✦ ✦

Spruce up your pooch's abode: transform a dull and boring canine kennel into the most desirable doggy digs in the country.

YOU WILL NEED

- Wooden dog house, flatpack or premade
- Sandpaper
- Latex paint, for base coat and stencils
- Three letter-size sheets of thin cardboard for stencils
- Thick, dry stencil paintbrush
- Fine paintbrush
- Matt wood varnish
- Gold letters

✶ If you are using a flatpack doghouse, assemble it according to the manufacturer's instructions. Lightly sand all surfaces for a smooth paint surface.

✶ Apply a base coat to the exterior walls and roof. Leave to dry.

✶ Using the templates on page 137, cut out negative dog shapes in three different sizes and a positive flower shape in one size from the cardboard.

✶ Holding the stencil in position on the walls or roof, dab the paint through the cardboard with a stencil paintbrush. Repeat to make the desired pattern. Paint on more detail, such as a scallop edge, with a fine paintbrush.

✶ Once dry, apply a thin coat of wood varnish. Spell out the occupant's name in gold letters above the door.

TOTO'S DOG JACKET

✦ ✦

Toto truly is a show-off, and why not? With a jacket like this, your pup will be the most handsome of hounds. The fleece lining makes it the perfect winter coat for any dandy dog.

YOU WILL NEED

- Tape measure
- 1-yard square of print fabric
- 1-yard square of fleece fabric
- 2 yards of ³/₄"-wide bias binding, in matching color to print fabric
- 4" of hook-and-loop fastening tape
- Matching sewing threads
- Appliqué sequin stars

✳ First, measure the lucky dog for its new jacket. You need the following measurements: the loose circumference around the widest part of the neck (A); the distance between the nape of the neck and the base of the tail (B); the circumference around the widest part of the chest (C).

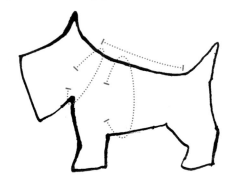

✳ Using the template on page 137, enlarge the shape to create a bespoke jacket based on your dog's measurements: the curved inner neckline should be the same as measurement A. The length from the neckline to the tail end should be the same as B. The width should be the same as C but less 10". Draw a paper pattern and double-check it by holding it against the dog.

✳ Using the paper pattern, cut one jacket shape from both the print and fleece fabrics. Place the two jacket pieces with wrong sides together and all raw edges aligned. Pin and baste. Starting at the center of the lower edge, finish the outside edge with bias binding, stitching it down by hand or machine. Ease the binding around the curved corners, stretching it gently (1).

✳ To make the strap, cut a 2¹/₂"-x-12" rectangle from both the print and fleece fabrics. Place the pieces together and edge with bias binding as before.

✳ Position one end of the strap in the center of one side edge. Pin it to the underside of the jacket, about 2" from the edge. Work reinforcing stitching over the end by sewing a square with a cross inside.

✳ Cut a ⁵/₈"-x-1¹/₄" piece of hook-and-loop tape for the neck and a 2"-x-2" piece for the waist. Separate the tape into hook pieces and loop pieces. Stitch the separate pieces on either side of the neck opening, one on the topside facing upward and the other on the underside facing downward. Repeat for the strap with one on the topside of the jacket and one on the underside of the strap (2).

✳ Trim with ultraglam appliqué sequin stars.

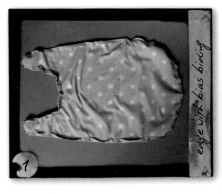

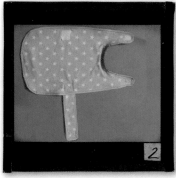

Finest Peanut Butter
TOTO'S TREATS

★ ★

Give your own very special dog an occasional treat with
Toto's favorite peanut butter cookie snacks.

YOU WILL NEED

- 1 1/3 cups whole-wheat flour
- 1 1/3 cups all-purpose flour
- 3/4 cup plus 2 tablespoons water
- 2 1/2 ounces peanut butter
- 2 tablespoons vegetable oil
- Bone-shaped cookie cutter

Makes 30–40 treats

✴ Preheat the oven to 350°F.

✴ In a large bowl, sift together the whole-wheat flour and all-purpose flour. Add the water, peanut butter, and vegetable oil, then mix well to form a thick dough.

✴ If the dough is too dry, add a few more drops of water to loosen.

✴ On a floured surface, roll out the dough to a thickness of about 1/4". Using a cookie cutter, press out bone shapes. Reroll all the scraps of dough to make more treats.

✴ Place on ungreased baking sheets. Bake in the oven for 20 minutes. Depending on the size of your oven, bake in batches.

"DOROTHY PUT ON A GREEN
SILK APRON AND TIED A
GREEN RIBBON AROUND
TOTO'S NECK, AND THEY
STARTED FOR THE THRONE
ROOM OF THE GREAT OZ. "

~ Chapter 11 ~
The Wonderful Emerald City of Oz

THE GREAT WIZARD'S
THRONE TENT

Create your own spectacular tent, one fit for the Great Oz himself! This throne tent is perfect for a child's bedroom or as an extravagant set dressing for a Moroccan-style party.

YOU WILL NEED

- 3¼ yards of 44"-wide satin fabric in each of white, emerald, and navy
- 4½ yards of ⅜"-wide ribbon
- Small plastic hula hoop, about 24" in diameter
- Lengths of rickrack and pom-pom trims in various sizes and colors
- Appliqué flowers

"DOROTHY FOUND HERSELF IN A WONDERFUL PLACE. A BIG, ROUND ROOM WITH A HIGH ARCHED ROOF, THE WALLS AND CEILING AND FLOOR WERE COVERED WITH LARGE EMERALDS SET CLOSELY TOGETHER."

~ Chapter 11 ~
The Wonderful City of Oz

✶ Cut a 44"-x-20" piece off one end of each length of satin, shortening them each to 97". Set aside the 20" pieces for the tent roof.

✶ Lay the 97" lengths of satin out flat on a clean floor with the longest sides at the top and bottom. Measure and mark the points 12" down from the top left edge and 12" up from the bottom right edge. Stretch a piece of string taut across the satin from these two marked points to give a guide for the cutting line (1). Cut the satin along the marked diagonal. You now have six panels.

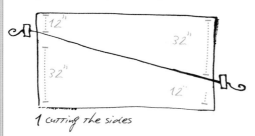

1 cutting the sides

✶ Place the long straight edge of a navy panel and the long diagonal edge of a white panel with right sides together and raw top edges aligned. Stitch with a ⅜" seam allowance. As the diagonal edge is longer than the straight edge, an amount of satin will be unstitched at the bottom edge. Repeat for the remaining panels, alternating colors. Turn under and stitch a ⅜" hem along the long raw edges of the first and last panels.

✶ Once all the panels are joined, trim away the unstitched excess at the bottom to create a neat curved edge. Turn under and stitch a ⅜" hem along this bottom edge.

✶ From each of the 20" pieces of satin, cut two 12" equilateral triangles. With right sides together, sew together these triangles to form a circle. Stitch with a ⅜" seam allowance. Before stitching the final seam, add the hanging loop by folding an 8" length of ribbon in half and inserting it into the seam at the center of the circle (2). Stitch the seam to complete the circular tent roof.

✶ Place the roof and main panels with right sides together, aligning the raw edges and matching the seams. Stitch together with a ⅜" seam allowance.

✶ Cut twelve 4" lengths of ribbon and hand stitch two to the wrong side at each seam junction. Turn the tent right side out and place the hula hoop in position where the roof and panels meet. Tie the ribbon pairs into bows to hold the hoop in place.

✶ Sew two 26" lengths of ribbon to both front panels for tiebacks. Decorate with any embellishments, such as rickrack, pom-pom trims, and ready-made appliqué flowers.

Illuminating! Enlightening!

THE AMAZING STAR OF OZ

★ ★

Bring a little bit of showmanship to any room with this illuminated star.

YOU WILL NEED

- 22"-x-34" sheet of 1/8"-thick foam-core board
- 22"-x-34" sheet of thin silver cardboard
- Spray adhesive or white craft glue
- Electric drill and drill bit roughly the same diameter as the lightbulbs
- Wooden spoon with round-ended handle
- Metal ruler
- Craft knife and cutting mat
- String of 20 miniature lights with removable lightbulbs
- Hot-glue gun
- Masking tape

Caution: Do not leave the lights unattended when switched on.

To make the star

★ Cut out a 16" square of both foam-core board and silver cardboard. Glue the silver cardboard to the foam-core board.

★ Using the template on page 138, trace the star onto the wrong side of the foam-core board. (From point to point, the star should be 15 1/2" long.) Transfer all the markings.

★ Using an electric drill, make a hole through the foam-core board at each of the 20 points marked on the template.

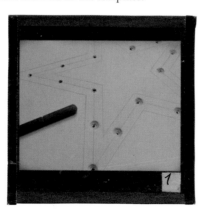

★ Press the round-ended handle of a wooden spoon into each of the drilled holes to indent the foam-core board. Press the handle down as firmly as you can (1).

★ Carefully cut out the star using a metal ruler, craft knife, and cutting mat. Apply a little extra glue at each point of the star to make sure the silver cardboard is firmly fixed to the foam-core board.

★ Remove each lightbulb from the string of lights. Starting at one point of the star, place the first socket in the hole from the back of the board. Repeat for all 20 sockets (2). Push the lightbulbs back into the sockets from the silver side through the board. Make sure the holes are large enough or the lightbulbs and sockets will not properly connect (3).

insert the lightbulb sockets

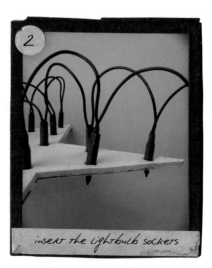

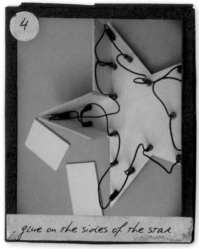

glue on the sides of the star

For the sides of the star

✶ Cut ten 3¹/₄"-x-5" rectangles from the foam-core board. Working your way around the star, glue one rectangle to each side of the star using a hot-glue gun. For added support, use masking tape to hold the sides in place. At the star point that holds the final light before the plug, leave a gap for the cord to fit through. Don't worry if your rectangles don't join up perfectly as this will be covered up in the next step.

✶ Measure the length of each side of the star. They should be 6"; if not, adjust the length of the rectangle cut in the next step accordingly.

✶ Cut one 3¹/₄"-x-60" strip from the silver cardboard. (Make this single long strip from two 30"-long strips). Draw a line every 6" (or the length of the sides of your star) along this

rectangle. Score along each of these lines to create a sharp crease.

✶ Glue the cardboard strip to the sides of the star, neatly butting up to the front edge. The creases will fall in place at the points of the star.

✶ Cut a small hole in the silver side and feed through the electrical cord.

WHICH WITCH ❧ ARE YOU? ❧

Answer the following questions to determine whether you are a graceful Glinda or a menacing Mombi.

1. IF YOU HAD TO LIVE IN A CERTAIN PART OF THE COUNTRY WOULD IT BE...
A: THE EAST OR WEST
B: THE NORTH OR SOUTH

2. WOULD YOU SAY THE POWER OF GOOD WAS STRONGER THAN THE POWER OF EVIL?
A: NO B: YES

3. WHEN YOU LAUGH DO YOU...
A: HAVE A GOOD CACKLE
B: POLITELY CHIRP, COVERING YOUR MOUTH WITH YOUR HAND

4. HOW MANY EYES DO YOU HAVE?
A: 1 B: 2

5. IF YOU HAD TO HAVE A PET WOULD IT BE...
A: A MONKEY, IDEALLY ONE THAT COULD FLY
B: I DON'T HAVE PETS, AS I AM TOO DELICATE AND ALLERGIC

6. ON A FUN NIGHT OUT WOULD YOU PREFER TO...
A: COMMAND YOUR MONKEY ARMY TO DESTROY ALL TRESPASSERS ON YOUR LAND
B: FLOAT AROUND IN A BUBBLE OF LOVELINESS

7. WHEN SHAPING YOUR NAILS, DO YOU FIND THAT...
A: YOU NEED TO CLIP THEM WITH GARDEN SHEARS, AS THEY ARE SO TOUGH
B: BUFFING WITH A SIMPLE NAIL FILE WILL SUFFICE

8. YOUR FAVORITE DRESS IS...
A: DEFINETLY THE BLACK ONE WITH THE HIGH COLLAR AND MATCHING CAPE
B: I CAN'T DECIDE, THERE ARE SO MANY, OH, I DON'T KNOW... SOMETHING PINK

RESULTS

MOSTLY As
My, oh, my. You are a dastardly witch, through and through. You have a very devious streak and a taste for the alternative. Your tattered clothes, threatening nature, struggle for power, and cackle give you away as a person to avoid.

MOSTLY Bs
What a goodie-two-shoes you are. A delicate and pretty thing who scares easily, you love to sing and dance—sometimes to the annoyance of others. Looking in the mirror is one of your favorite pastimes, because you are just so perfect.

EVEN NUMBER OF As & Bs
You are the perfect mix of good and bad; the best way to be. You have the beauty of a good witch with the sassiness and attitude of a bad witch.

I'm melting! WITCH CANDLES

✶ ✶

Use a cookie cutter to make these ingenious candles and watch your wicked witch disappear in a puff of smoke. These candles look great flying together as a coven.

YOU WILL NEED

- Paraffin wax pellets or beads
- Tin can or metal jug
- Old saucepan
- Black candle dye in chips or pellets
- Medium lead-free wire wick
- Plastic jug
- Baking sheet with sides
- Baking parchment paper
- Witch-shaped cookie cutter
- Black table candles
- Wooden toothpicks (or wooden cocktail sticks)

✶ Place the wax pellets or beads in a tin can or metal jug. Place the tin can in an old saucepan, if necessary resting on a trivet. Fill the saucepan with cold water to just below the rim of the can or jug. Bring the water to a boil, then turn the heat down to a simmer until the wax melts. When the wax is molten, add some black candle dye.

✶ Line the baking sheet with parchment paper. Pour the black wax into the lined baking sheet, leaving a small amount in the can or jug. Let the wax cool until it is pliable and soft to the touch.

✶ Using the cookie cutter, press out two witch shapes per candle and peel away from the parchment. Place a length of wick on the inside of one wax shape, starting at the bottom of the witch and extending beyond the top of her hat. Lay a wooden toothpick on the bottom third of the wax shape (1).

✶ Using the left-over wax, stick the second wax witch shape on top of the first, matching

insert the wick & toothpick

up the contours and sandwiching the wick and toothpick in between. Leave to cool.

✶ Cut the tops of the black table candles and place in a microwave for 10 seconds to soften the wax.

✶ Make a hole in the top of each table candle by skewering with a wooden toothpick. Position the witch-shaped candles in the tops of the table candles by slotting the toothpick into the hole.

"SHE PICKED UP THE BUCKET OF WATER THAT STOOD NEAR AND DASHED IT OVER THE WITCH, WETTING HER FROM HEAD TO FOOT...INSTANTLY THE WICKED WOMAN GAVE A LOUD CRY OF FEAR, AND THEN, AS DOROTHY LOOKED AT HER IN WONDER, THE WITCH BEGAN TO SHRINK AND FALL AWAY.

~ Chapter 12 ~
The Search for the Wicked Witch

"'We will carry you,' replied the King, and no sooner had he spoken than two of the Monkeys caught Dorothy in their arms and flew away with her. Others took the Scarecrow and the Woodman and the Lion, and one little Monkey seized Toto and flew after them, although the dog tried hard to bite him."

~ Chapter 14 ~
The Winged Monkeys

PARTY

Winged Monkey
PARTY INVITES
✶ ✶
Send your very own troop of winged monkeys to deliver news of your fabulous party!

YOU WILL NEED

For each invitation card:
- 8¹⁄₂" x 11" of patterned thin scrapbook cardboard
- 8¹⁄₂" x 11" of thin silver cardboard
- 4" x 4³⁄₄" of thin white cardboard
- Rubber alphabet stamps

✶ Using the templates on page 138, cut out one body from each piece of patterned cardboard and two wings for each body from silver cardboard.

✶ Crease each wing along the dotted line marked on the template. Glue the wings to the body where indicated on the template.

✶ Fold the piece of white cardboard in half lengthwise. Print your party message on this card, using the rubber stamps. Write any other details inside the card by hand. Glue the card to the hands of your monkey.

Little Monkey's
BABY'S
BATH TOWEL

✶ ✶

*This cuddly bath towel is just right for all the little monkeys out there.
For a newborn baby, cut a 20" square from the towel and adjust the
size of all the other pieces accordingly.*

YOU WILL NEED

- Brown bath towel
- 3 yards of bias binding or velvet ribbon, about ¾" wide
- Beige hand towel
- 20" x 20" of yellow cotton fabric
- Black felt for eyes
- Matching sewing threads
- Brown and pink embroidery thread
- 16" x 20" of polyester batting
- Red wool pom-pom
- Appliqué sequin stars

✶ Cut a 29½" square from the brown bath towel. At three points of the square, round off the corners to a gentle curve.

✶ Starting and stopping about 8" along from the square corner, finish the outside edge with bias binding, stitching it down by hand or machine. Ease the binding around the curved corners, stretching it gently (1). If you are using velvet ribbon, fold it in half lengthwise first and press.

bind the raw towel edges

To make the monkey's face

✶ Cut a triangle, 17¼" x 11¾" x 11¾", from the brown bath towel. If possible, use the natural selvage as the longest straight side of the triangle. If this isn't possible, hem the edge to prevent fraying.

✶ Using the template on page 139, cut one muzzle from the beige towel. Embroider onto the muzzle a wide mouth in brown thread with chain stitch and two small nostrils in pink thread with straight stitch. With the longest edge of the triangle at the bottom, position the muzzle to create the monkey's face. Pin and stitch in place. Sew on two 1¼" black felt circles for eyes.

✶ Using the template on page 139, cut two inner ears from yellow cotton.

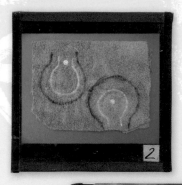

2

3

4

Place them right side up on a scrap of brown towel, 4" apart. Zigzag stitch around the edges. Using the outer ear template, trace the outlines onto the wrong side of the towel, with a ³/₄" margin all the way around the stitching lines (2).

✶ Place this scrap of towel on top of a second piece, with right sides together. Stitch around the outlines, leaving an opening at the base of each ear. Trim the excess fabric close to the lines of stitching. Turn right side out. Pinch the base of the ears together and secure with a few hand stitches (3).

✶ Lay out the large square of brown towel with the unbound square corner at the top. Position the ears at the top, one on each side about 4" down from the corner facing into the square. Place the monkey's face on top, with right sides together and raw edges aligned (4). Machine stitch making a curve at the corner. If your machine cannot stitch through all the layers at the ears, leave that section unstitched and then sew it by hand. Zigzag stitch all the raw edges to prevent fraying and trim any excess fabric. Turn right side out. The ears will pop into place.

For the monkey's wings
✶ Pin together 16¹/₂"-x-20" pieces of beige towel and yellow cotton, with right sides together. Using the wing template on page 139, trace one outline onto the wrong side of the cotton. Flip the template over and trace a second outline. Stitch, leaving openings where marked on the template. Trim the excess fabric close to the lines of stitching. Turn right side out.

✶ Using the same template, cut out two wing-shaped pieces of batting. Feed the batting into the wings, trimming if necessary for a good fit (5).

✶ To quilt the wings, topstitch along the dotted lines marked on the template.

✶ Neatly close the opening on each wing with small neat hand stitches. Stitch the wings in place on the back of the towel, 10" down from the hood.

✶ Decorate with a red pom-pom on the point of the hood and appliqué sequin stars on the front edges.

THE LION THOUGHT IT MIGHT BE AS WELL TO FRIGHTEN THE WIZARD, SO HE GAVE A LARGE, LOUD ROAR, WHICH WAS SO FIERCE AND DREADFUL THAT TOTO JUMPED AWAY FROM HIM IN ALARM AND TIPPED OVER THE SCREEN THAT STOOD IN A CORNER. AS IT FELL WITH A CRASH THEY LOOKED THAT WAY, AND THE NEXT MOMENT ALL OF THEM WERE FILLED WITH WONDER.

I THINK YOU ARE A

VERY BAD MAN

FOR THEY SAW, STANDING IN JUST THE SPOT THE SCREEN HAD HIDDEN, A LITTLE OLD MAN, WITH A BALD HEAD AND A WRINKLED FACE, WHO SEEMED TO BE AS MUCH SURPRISED AS THEY WERE. THE TIN WOODMAN, RAISING HIS AXE, RUSHED TOWARD THE LITTLE MAN AND CRIED OUT, "WHO ARE YOU?" "I AM OZ, THE GREAT AND TERRIBLE," SAID THE LITTLE MAN, IN A TREMBLING VOICE.

Said Dorothy

★ ★

OH NO MY DEAR, I'M REALLY A

VERY GOOD MAN

but I'm a ★★★★★★★★★★★★★★★★★★★★★★★★

VERY BAD WIZARD

WHAT DO YOU WISH FOR?

ONE GO ONLY

Follow the paths and help everyone find their goals, their dreams, and what they truly desire.

THE COWARDLY LION

"MY LIFE IS SIMPLY UNBEARABLE WITHOUT A BIT OF COURAGE."

TIN WOODMAN

"WHILE I WAS IN LOVE I WAS THE HAPPIEST MAN ON EARTH; BUT NO ONE CAN LOVE WHO HAS NOT A HEART."

THE SCARECROW
"IF MY HEAD STAYS STUFFED
WITH STRAW INSTEAD OF
BRAINS...HOW AM I TO
EVER KNOW ANYTHING?"

DOROTHY
"I AM ANXIOUS TO GET BACK
TO MY AUNT AND UNCLE,
FOR I AM SURE THEY WILL
WORRY ABOUT ME. CAN YOU
HELP ME FIND MY WAY?"

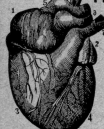

Oz Apothecary
SLEEPY-TIME SALT SCRUB WITH LAVENDER

This exfoliating sea-salt and lavender scrub works magic on even the witchiest of scaly skin!

YOU WILL NEED

- 4½ ounces coarse sea salt
- 4 heads dried lavender flowers
- 5 drops lavender essence
- 3½ tablespoons - olive oil
- Storage jar

Skin type: all

✻ Place all the ingredients together in a large bowl and mix thoroughly.

✻ Transfer to a glass storage jar with a lid with a tight seal. This scrub can be kept for up to two weeks.

How to use
✻ When bathing or showering, rub a handful of the scrub over your body to exfoliate any dead skin. Your skin will be left feeling ultramoisturized and soft.

Oz Apothecary
FACE MASK OF ETERNAL YOUTH

The banana is the secret to this oatmeal-and-honey face mask: a rich source of vitamins, an anti-inflammatory, and stuffed with antioxidants, it gives skin a supple, youthful glow.

YOU WILL NEED

- 1 banana
- 1 teaspoon honey
- ¼ teaspoon jojoba oil
- 3½ ounces rolled oats

Skin type: all

✻ Place the banana and the honey in a bowl. Mash together to form a paste. Add the jojoba oil. Stir in the oats.

How to use
✻ Apply liberally to a fully cleansed face, avoiding the eye area. Leave for 15 minutes. Rinse off with warm water. Your skin with be left rejuvenated and glowing.

Oz Apothecary

&ck "PUT A BRAVE FACE ON IT" &ck
SKIN TONIC

Not only does this delightfully aromatic tonic tone, it also calms and hydrates,
leaving your skin feeling ready to face the world once again.

YOU WILL NEED

- 20 fragrant rose heads
- 5 pints water
- Bag of ice cubes
- Two small heatproof bowls
- Large metal saucepan with lid

Skin type: normal–dry

✶ Separate the petals from the rose heads, discarding any stems and leaves. Rinse thoroughly in cold water.

✶ Place a small heatproof bowl upside down in the center of the saucepan. Scatter the rose petals around the bowl inside the saucepan. On top of the upside-down bowl, rest a second bowl the right way up.

✶ Pour enough water into the saucepan to just cover the rose petals. Do not pour any water into the bowls. Place the lid on the saucepan, but upside down.

✶ Turn on the heat and bring the water to a boil. Once boiling, reduce to a low heat and simmer for 5 minutes.

✶ Fill the inverted saucepan lid with ice cubes. The rosewater will collect in the bowl inside the saucepan: check every 10 minutes to see how much rosewater has collected. Replenish the melted ice. Stop this process once you have collected about 2 $\frac{1}{2}$ cups of rosewater. The entire process should take about 30 minutes.

✶ Transfer to a sterile container and allow to cool. This tonic can be kept for up to two weeks.

How to use
✶ To use as a toner, apply to the face after cleansing. Dab onto a cotton pad and gently wipe over the skin. This helps to refine pores, reduce puffiness, and moisturize.

✶ Rosewater can also be used as a make-up remover, an aftershave, to treat sunburn, to reduce swelling, to soothe a headache, and even in cooking.

The Wonderful Wizard's
BALLOON MOBILE

★ ★

The Wonderful Wizard escaped Oz in a hot-air balloon made from different pieces of green silk. These paper balloons waft gently in the breeze and are mesmerizing in a child's room.

YOU WILL NEED

- Various sheets of plain and patterned scrapbook paper: for the largest balloon, you will need enough sheets to cut thirty 10¼"-diameter circles. (The balloons work best if the paper is all of a similar thickness.)
- Craft knife or pair of scissors
- Pinking shears
- Double-sided adhesive tape
- Hot-glue gun or superglue
- Colored or metallic embroidery thread
- Gems, buttons, or paper shapes for extra decoration
- Awl and cutting mat
- Strong thread, such as button or bookbinding
- Large needle
- Invisible fishing wire

These paper balloons look beautiful swaying in the breeze and provide an unusual focal point when placed above a bed or hung in a group over a dining table. The following instructions are for the large green balloon shown in the photograph opposite. Enlarge or reduce the size of the circles and the basket to make larger or smaller balloons.

To make the basket

★ For the basket base, draw a 3½"-diameter circle on a sheet of paper and cut out with an extra ³/₈" all the way around. Score around the drawn circle with the blunt edge of a craft knife or pair of scissors. Make small snips into the outer ³/₈", about ¼" apart, around the circumference of the circle to make little tabs. Fold these tabs upward. For the basket sides, cut a 2½"-x-11¾" rectangle from the same paper. For a decorative edge, use pinking shears.

make the basket

★ Place double-sided adhesive tape along one long and one short edge of the rectangle. Peel off the backing papers. Join the sides to the base by fixing the rectangle to the cut tabs of the circle, pressing down each tab. Once attached to the base, press the short edges of the sides together to secure (1).

To make the swags

★ Using the template on page 139, trace the outline onto paper four times. Score along the middle line marked on the template.

Gently pinch each swag to make it 3-D (2).

★ Using a hot-glue gun, fix the swags evenly around the basket so they just touch, about ³/₈" down from the top edge. At the point where two swags meet, glue a 8" length of embroidery thread. Cover the join with a decorative gem, button, or paper shape.

To make the balloon

★ Cut out thirty to forty 10¼"-diameter circles from various colored and patterned papers. The more circles you use, the fuller

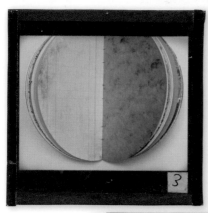

the balloon will be. For smaller balloons, use fewer paper circles.

⁎ Fold each circle in half. Make two equal stacks of semi circles. Place the two stacks next to each other to form a whole circle.

⁎ For the stitching guide, measure and mark the points 1¹/₂" down from the top edge and 1¹/₂" up from the bottom edge of each semi circle. Make another mark ³/₄" farther in. Repeat at the middle. For the hanging loop, using an awl make a hole ³/₈" down from the top edge of each stack of circles.

⁎ Take one of the stacks and open out the circles so they lay flat. Using an awl

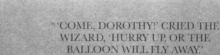

and a cutting mat, make holes at each mark through all the circles of paper. Using strong thread and a large needle, stitch the circles together. Repeat for the second stack of circles. Place one sewn stack on top of the other and stitch together to make one big stack. Make sure the first half of the circles bend one way, then the second half bend the other way.

⁎ Run a length of invisible fishing wire through the top hole. Suspend your balloon at a height where it is easy to work with. The paper leaves will naturally fan out to create a sphere.

⁎ Fix the basket to the balloon by stitching through a different paper leaf

for each string. Spend time finding the right leaves so the basket hangs straight. You can temporarily fix the basket strings in place with glue dots while experimenting with different positions.

⁎ Using the template on page 139, cut out bows from paper for the kite tails. Concertina the center of each bow and fix with a few hand stitches.

⁎ Add kite tails to the basket, decorated with strings of paper bows or small triangles to make bunting.

"'COME, DOROTHY!' CRIED THE WIZARD, 'HURRY UP, OR THE BALLOON WILL FLY AWAY.'

'I CAN'T FIND TOTO ANYWHERE,' REPLIED DOROTHY, WHO DID NOT WISH TO LEAVE HER LITTLE DOG BEHIND."

~ Chapter 17 ~
How the Balloon was Launched

THERE IS ♥ NO PLACE LIKE HOME

DRESS-UP DOROTHY & TOTO

enlarge by 200%

HAIR FRONT
cut one from brown felt

FACE FRONT
cut one from white cotton

HAIR BACK
cut one from brown felt

SHOES
cut four from red felt

COLLAR BACK
cut one

COLLAR FRONT
cut one

LEGS *cut four from striped cotton*

ARMS *cut four from white cotton*

BODY
cut two from gingham cotton

"DOROTHY HAD ONLY ONE OTHER
DRESS, IT WAS GINGHAM, WITH
CHECKS OF WHITE AND BLUE."

~ Chapter 3 ~
How Dorothy Saved the Scarecrow

LION HEAD
cut one each from yellow
and orange felt

LION EAR
cut two

LION MANE
cut one from
orange felt

LION MUZZLE
cut one from
cream felt

APRON
cut one from
gingham cotton

APRON POCKET
cut one

TOTO
cut two from
black felt

BASKET SIDES
cut two from
brown felt

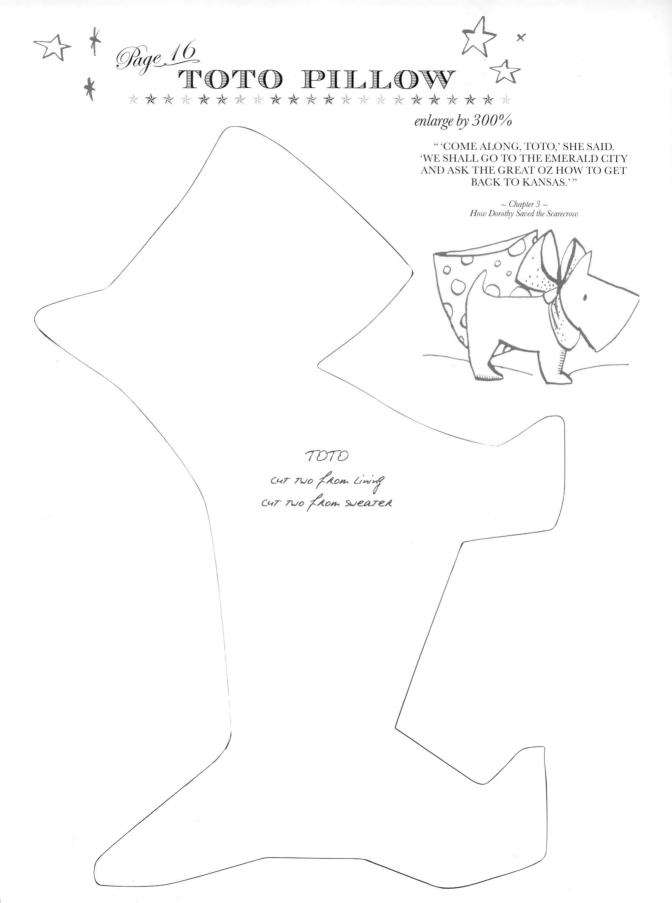

TOTO PILLOW

enlarge by 300%

" 'COME ALONG, TOTO,' SHE SAID.
'WE SHALL GO TO THE EMERALD CITY
AND ASK THE GREAT OZ HOW TO GET
BACK TO KANSAS.' "

~ Chapter 3 ~
How Dorothy Saved the Scarecrow

TOTO

cut two from lining

cut two from sweater

Page 36
MUNCHKIN HAT EGG COZIES

enlarge egg cozy by 120% *enlarge accessories by 200%*

HAT
CUT ONE

BRIM
CUT ONE

FLOWER PETALS CUT TWO

FLOWER CENTER
CUT ONE

FEATHER

Page 38
MUNCHKIN
PLACE CARDS

enlarge by 200%

GIRL
FACE

BOY
FACE

APRON

Page 34
GLINDA
DOLL

copy at 100%

THE NO-BRAINER SCARECROW

★ ★

enlarge in relation to your scarecrow sticks

COLLAR

CUT ONE

SCARECROW BODY

CUT TWO

"WHILE DOROTHY WAS LOOKING EARNESTLY
INTO THE QUEER, PAINTED FACE OF THE
SCARECROW, SHE WAS SURPRISED TO SEE ONE
OF THE EYES SLOWLY WINK AT HER."

~ Chapter 3 ~
How Dorothy Saved the Scarecrow

HEART GARLAND
★ ★

copy at 100%

HEART

cut as many
in each size
as you prefer

BIRD WING

cut two

A   B

BIRD

cut two

THE COWARDLY LION HAND PUPPET

★ ★

enlarge by 150%

A

BACK BODY
cut one from yellow felt

FRONT BODY
cut one from yellow felt

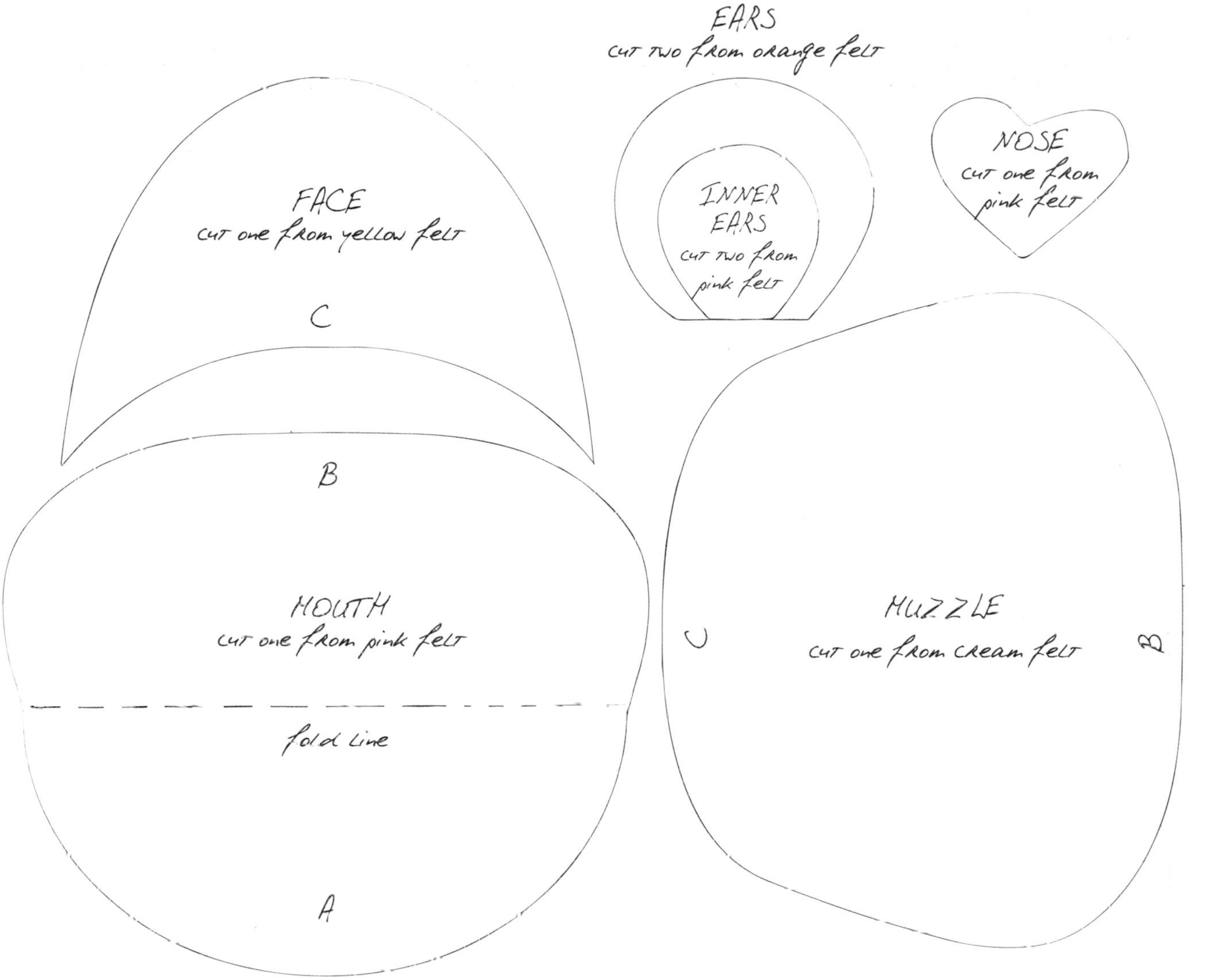

EARS
cut two from orange felt

INNER
EARS
cut two from
pink felt

NOSE
cut one from
pink felt

FACE
cut one from yellow felt

C

B

MOUTH
cut one from pink felt

- -

fold line

A

MUZZLE
cut one from cream felt

C

B

"THAT DOESN'T MAKE ME ANY BRAVER,
AND AS LONG AS I KNOW MYSELF TO BE
A COWARD I SHALL BE UNHAPPY."

~ Chapter 6 ~
The Cowardly Lion

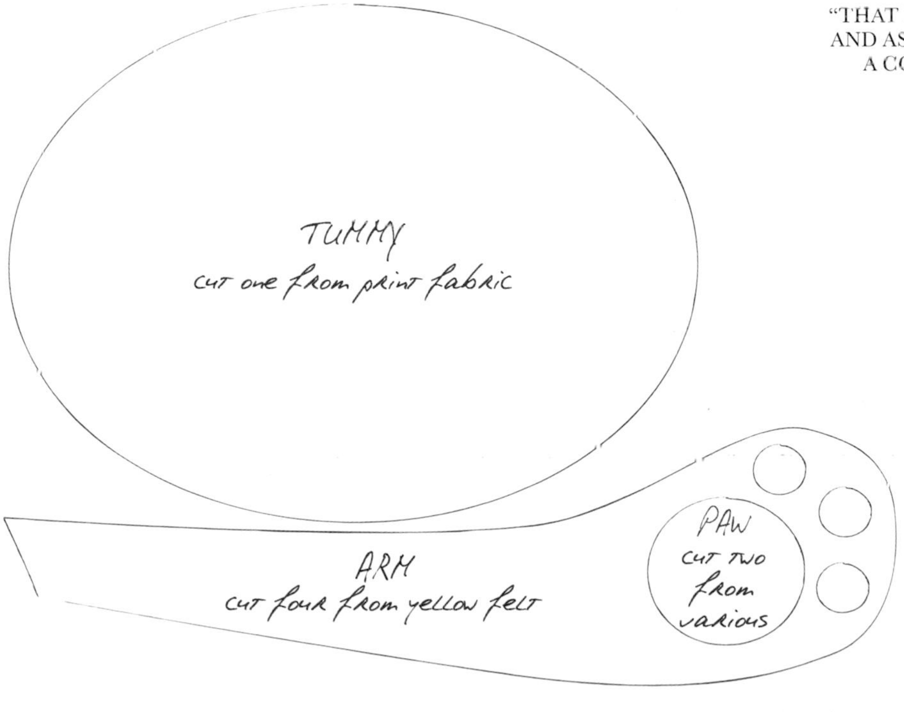

TUMMY
cut one from print fabric

PAW
cut two
from
various

ARM
cut four from yellow felt

FIELD O' POPPIES

enlarge by 225%

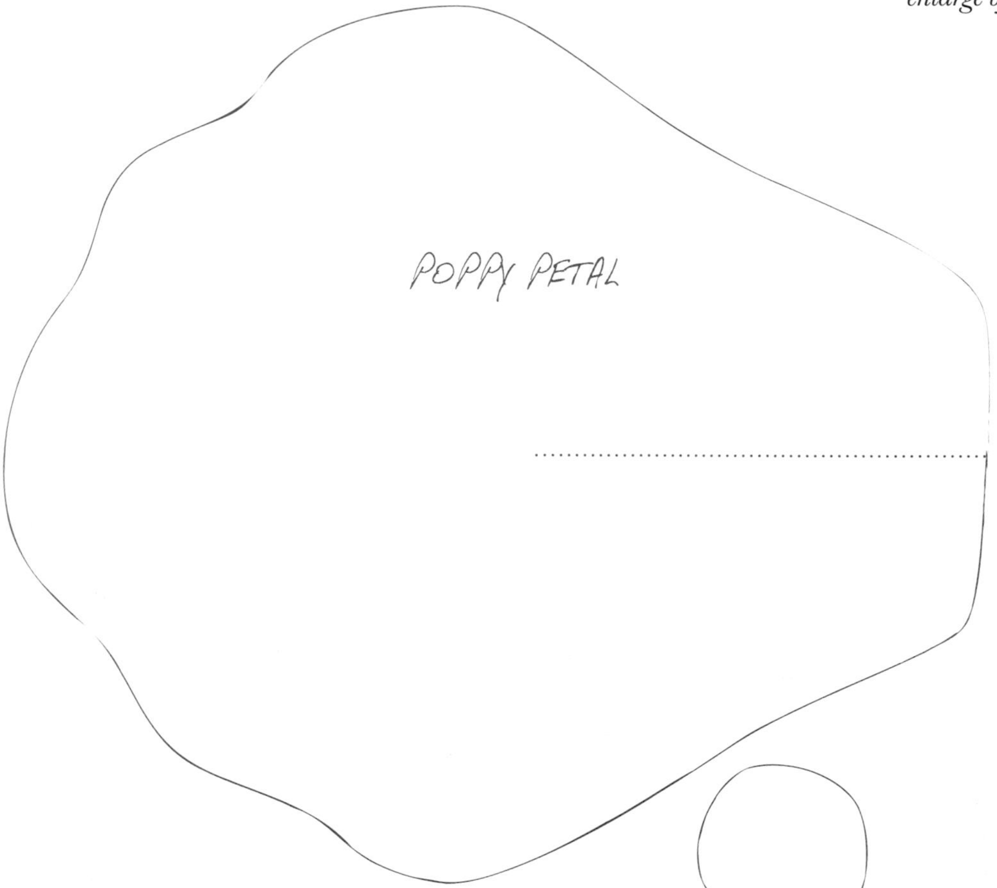

POPPY PETAL

"THEY NOW CAME UPON
MORE AND MORE OF THE
BIG SCARLET POPPIES,
AND FEWER OF THE
OTHER FLOWERS.

~ Chapter 8 ~
The Deadly Poppy Field

POPPY STAMEN

SLEEPY-TIME EYEMASK

enlarge by 110%

A

B

EYEMASK
cut one from each silk fabric and cut one from soft velour (lining fabric)

EMBROIDERY GUIDE

● Running Stitch   ● Straight Stitch   ● Split Stitch   ● French knot

Divide the thread of the preceding stitch with the needle when entering material

EMERALD HAIRPIECES

✳ ✳

copy at 100%

Page 78

PATCHWORK PICNIC SET

✳ ✳

enlarge by 300%

DECORATED DOGHOUSE

enlarge to suit your dog house

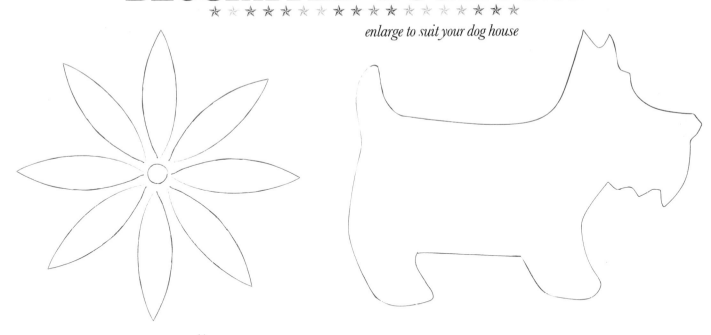

TOTO'S DOG JACKET

enlarge to fit your dog

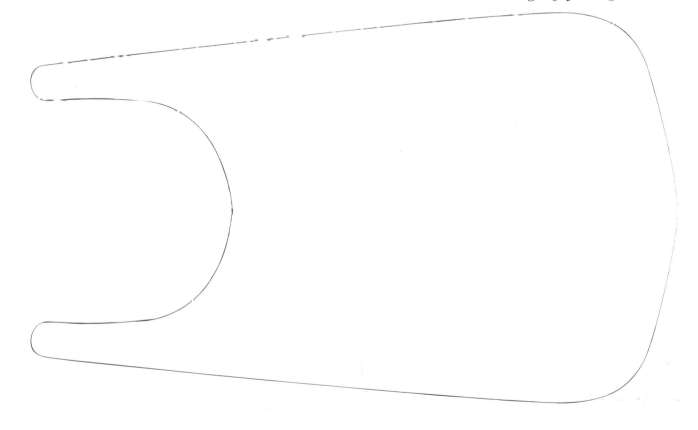

THE AMAZING STAR OF OZ

enlarge by 400%

STAR
cut one from
foam-core board
and thin silver
cardboard

WINGED MONKEY PARTY INVITES

enlarge by 200%

MONKEY WING
cut two from thin silver
cardboard

MONKEY BODY
cut one from
patterned paper

Page 112 BABY'S BATH TOWEL

enlarge by 200%

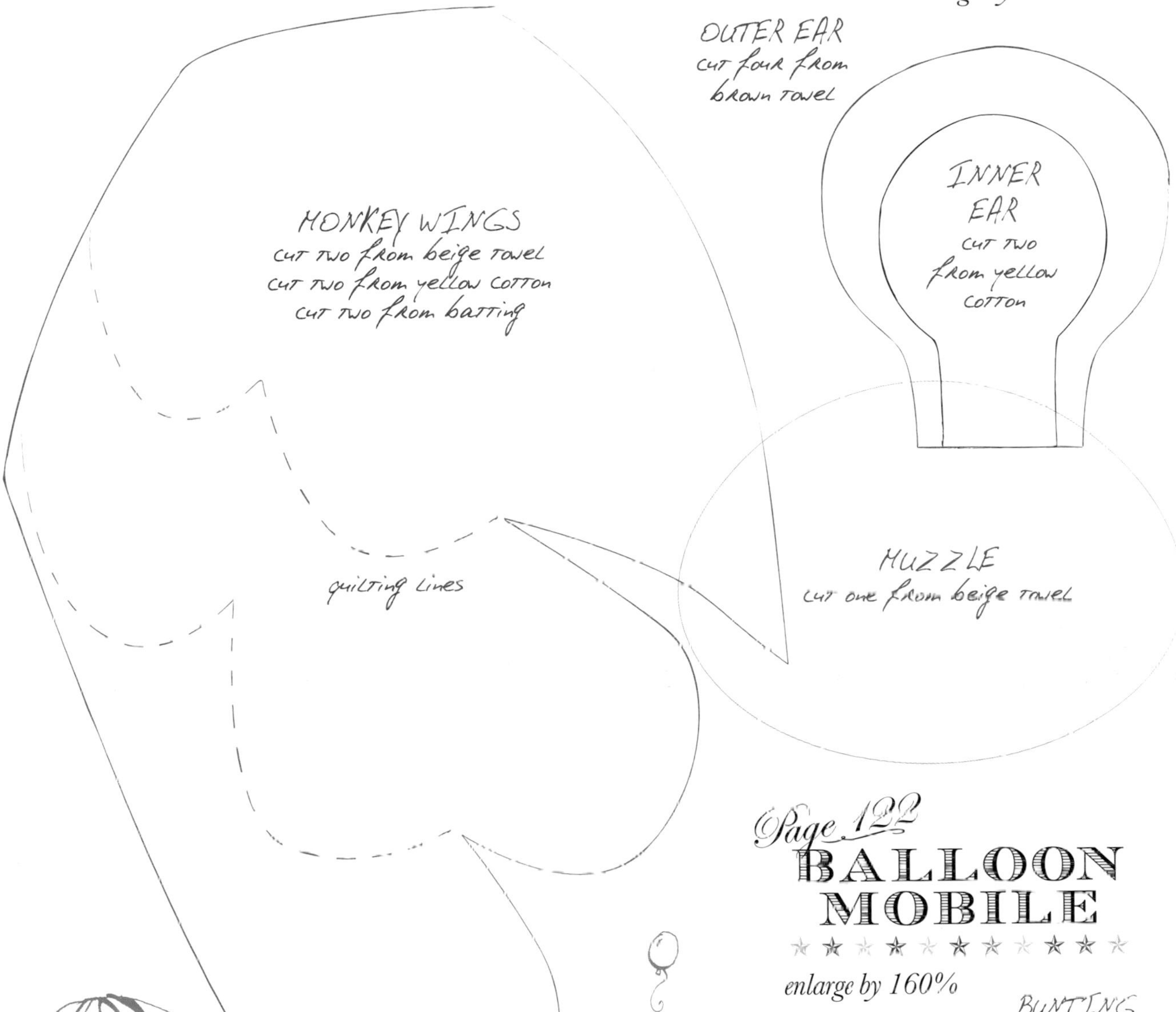
OUTER EAR
cut four from
brown towel
INNER
EAR
cut two
from yellow
cotton
MONKEY WINGS
cut two from beige towel
cut two from yellow cotton
cut two from batting
quilting lines
MUZZLE
cut one from beige towel

Page 122 BALLOON MOBILE

enlarge by 160%

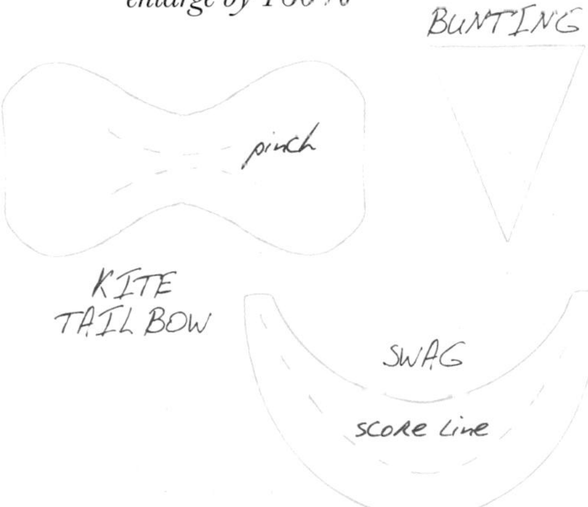
BUNTING
pinch
KITE
TAIL BOW
SWAG
score line

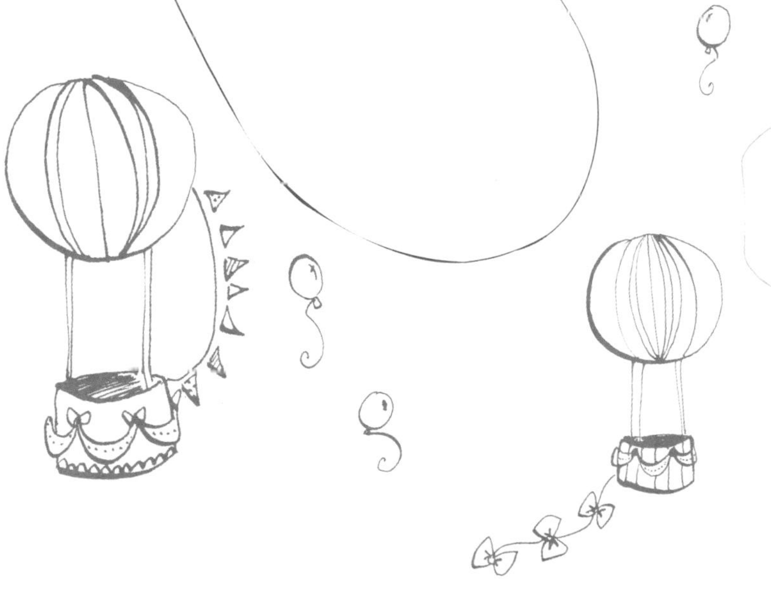

DIRECTORY

SUPPLIERS

Cooking utensils and cooking ingredients

If you are looking for cooking utensils, pans, or specialty ingredients, try the following:

Amazon
Amazon is a good source for a surprising array of cake-baking

supplies and ingredients.
www.amazon.com

Williams Sonoma
For bakeware and specialty cake ingredients.
www.williams-sonoma.com

Wilton
Specialty cake decorating store. Good for ready-to-use rolled

fondant, food colorings, edible glitter, and cake and cupcake pans.
www.wilton.com

Ultimate Baker
For cake-baking supplies and specialty ingredients.
www.cooksdream.com

Fabrics and Notions

For general and specialty fabrics, felts, and sewing notions and tools, try these suppliers:

A Child's Dream Come True
For 100% wool felt in 61 colors and plant-dyes felt in 15 colors.
www.achildsdream.com

Born to Quilt
Stores that sell quilting fabrics like this one offer a wide range of cotton print fabrics.
www.borntoquilt.com

Fabric Depot
A large online store offering quilting fabrics, general fabrics, and sewing notions.
www.fabricdepot.com

fabric.com
For general fabrics.
www.fabric.com

Fat Quarter Shop
For cotton print fabrics in small quantities.
www.fatquartershop.com

Felt-o-rama
Source of 100% wool German felt and wool-blend felt.
www.feltorama.com

Free Spirit Fine Quilting Fabric
For designer quilting fabrics.
www.freespiritfabric.com

Jo-Ann
Use the store locator at the online site to find a store near you. Jo-Ann carries fabrics, toy stuffing, beads, jewelry supplies, embroidery threads, and sewing notions and tools.
www.joann.com

Reprodepot Fabrics
Offers fabrics with vintage and retro themes.
www.reprodepotfabrics.com

General craft

Try the following general craft stores for a wide range of craft supplies for painting, scrapbooking, paper craft, and so on.

Jo-Ann
See Fabrics and Notions.

Michaels Stores
Has supplies for paper craft, scrapbooking, and sewing.
www.michaels.com

Millinery Supplies

Try your local craft store for millinery supplies such as sinamay fabric, or search online.

From the Neck Up
This site has a good list of millinery suppliers.
www.hatbook.com

Vintage ware

Visiting eBay is a brilliant way to snap up bargains on vintage china. Remember to look for pretty brands such as Shelly, Tuscan China, Foley, and Wedgwood.
www.ebay.com

Trimmings, Beads, and Buttons

Most fabric stores sell a selection of trimmings, beads, and buttons, but for a wider range, try the following:

M & J Trimming
This store in New York City has a huge range of cords, braids, buttons, and trimmings of all sorts.
www.mjtrim.com

Shipwreck Beads
For a wide range of beads.
www.shipsreckbeads.com

"'I HAVE COME FOR MY COURAGE,' ANNOUNCED THE LION, ENTERING THE ROOM."

~ Chapter 16 ~
The Magic Art of the Great Humbug

INSPIRATION

MUSEUMS

If you are a die-hard Oz fan, why not be adventurous and book a trip to visit Kansas, the setting for the story?

The Oz Museum

In the heart of Kansas, this museum is the place to go for all Oz fans.
511 Lincoln
Wamego, KS 66547
(866) 458-TOTO
www.ozmuseum.com

Land of Oz

An Oz-based theme park that is available both for parties and small private tours.
2669 Beech Mountain Parkway
Beech Mountain, NC 28604
(828 387-2000)
www.emeraldmtn.com

THEATER AND FILM

Why not get inspired and have a good old-fashioned sing-along by seeing these fantastic adaptations of the Oz story?

The Wizard of Oz

(1939, MGM) This film is a timeless classic starring Judy Garland.

Wizard of Oz

Based on the MGM film, this musical is great fun for the family.
www.wizardofozthemusical.com

Wicked

This musical tells the witches' story before we meet them in the book. Filled with fantastic original songs, it is well worth seeing.
www.wickedthemusical.com

BLOGS

everythingozbook.blogspot.com
theozenthusiast.blogspot.com
thewizardofozblog.com
ozmapolitan.wordpress.com

Christine blogs at
sewyeah.co.uk
and Hannah at
couturecraft.blogspot.co.uk

★ ★

WITH THANKS

Our sincerest thanks to L. Frank Baum for writing The Wizard of Oz. *To Mr. & Mrs. Peters for their kindness in sharing their farm with us. To Verity the Chicken Catcher. To Lisa, Nikki, James, Jane, Alison, and all at Quadrille Publishing for their continuing support. To Jan at HobbyCraft Plc for kindly sponsoring the fabric used in this book.*

Christine *Thank you again to everyone for their support during the making of the book, especially to Mum and Dad with their location scouting and kindly opening their house to us. To Aunty and Uncle for their advice on everything… To Nanny and Grandad for just being them. To Jo, Ian, Oliver & Elliot. To Joe and Joel and all the other Buzzers, fun times. To Jake, Kirsty, and Laura for keeping me sane. Love you all.*

Hannah *My darling Brendan, thank you for once again putting up with all my crafty behavior in our home. To Mum & Dad for taking me repeatedly to see our friend Charlie in* The Wizard of Oz *as a child. To Charlie Drake for gifting me his favorite book,* Down the Yellow Brick Road *by Doug McClelland. A big thank you to both Antonia—mummy to Maggie, our Toto—as well as Anna & James— parents of Christian, our flying monkey—for letting them model for us!*

★ ★